KV-540-043

Kitchener Blue

Alex Martinez

OPEN GATE PRESS
London

First published in 1996 by Open Gate Press
51 Achilles Road, London NW6 1DZ

Copyright © 1996 by Alex Martinez
All rights, by all media, reserved.

British Library Cataloguing-in-Publication Programme
A catalogue record for this book is available from the British
Library

ISBN: 1 871871 28 X

This is a work of fiction. Any resemblance to any person,
living or dead, is entirely coincidental.

Printed in Great Britain by
Redwood Books, Trowbridge, Wiltshire

To Ralph,
who took part in one
of the best Spanish classes
I ever had!
All best wishes,
Alea   Feb. 97

To my daughter Francesca, whose utter dread of
thunderstorms and fireworks belies the fact that she is a
true battler at heart and an example to many.

One

In October 1910, the unseasonally-cold weather notwithstanding, Jack Spencer Kitchener looked anything but blue. The friendly, neatly-cropped oval of his face still bore the stamp of youthful optimism, for although tailored to his modest expectations, the future seemed as rosy as his beloved wife's cheeks on the day she broke the news to him.

Jack and Rose had become the darlings of the high road in a matter of months. Their good looks, endearing shyness, and, paradoxically, their open affection for one another had proved so irresistible a combination that an admiring wash of "Donnit do yer' ear' good", "Donnay make a luvly couple" and "God bless 'em" was left in their wake whenever they strolled along the busy thoroughfare hand in hand. The same was true when, arms interlaced, the charming pair glided effortlessly across the polished floor of the Rockhall Parade Skating Rink in Cricklewood Broadway, aided and abetted by the musical wizardry of Professor Voorzanger's band. "Bloomin' marvellous!", condensing here and there in the winter months like little puffs of smoke, was among the most popular of accolades uttered by fellow skaters and enthusiastic rinkside observers.

The Rockhall Parade Rink held a very special place in their hearts, for it was there, in the early autumn of 1909, that Mr Kitchener proposed to Miss Langdon. Her timid but undeniably joyous 'yes' was scarcely audible above the rousing crescendos issuing triumphantly from the tip of the professor's baton. However, the measured tightening of her grip upon his hand, and the added lustre discernible in her eyes left him in absolutely

1

no doubt as to the nature of her reply. To no one's surprise, they were married the following summer at St Mary's, Priory Road. The best man was Ernest V. Laurence, stooping confectioner, friend, and, most importantly, at least where the married couple's material prospects were concerned, Jack's employer.

Yes, in the tenth month of 1910, Jack Kitchener looked anything but blue. Far from it. A stronger embrace than usual, preceded and followed by a lingering kiss, had welcomed him home from work on that cold autumn evening.

"Wha's go' into *you*?"

"Jack, I'm...expectin'!"

A gasp of disbelief; a tender placing of hands on now maternal midriff. "Are you sure?" he asks, still cupping the magical area in vain search of a confirmation.

"As sure as a woman can be."

And slowly but surely, the stroked, gently patted and carefully-monitored extension of flesh begins to swell, and with it the dreams and speculations of imminent parenthood.

"Wha' we gonna call it, Jack?"

"I though' we'd call it Frank if it's a boy, after 'is grandad, an' Rose if it's a girl."

"Jack!"

"Save those blushes, luv, it's gonna be a boy – you wai' an' see."

Growing ("Wha's 'e gonna be?" "Rich."). Getting bigger ("Gas cookers are much bet'er than coal fire, Jack."). Kicking ("Children's coats are 2/11 at Briglands, in the sale.").

Five and a half weeks before the coveted day, Jack Kitchener is still smiling with youthful optimism. It is Sunday, and High Road Kilburn is a sea of motionless vehicles. Hooting, ringing, and plaintive cries can be heard issuing from hundreds of motor cars and omnibuses. As though that were not enough noise for a peaceful Sunday morning, distressed carriage-drawing horses add their piercing whines to the general din. The pavements have vanished under an extended wave of people excitedly watching, commenting, pointing... As a May sky glares down with enviable indifference, the first stones are hurled at the suffragettes.

Jack shares a joke with Mr Laurence as the women's meeting is cut short by a group of irate high road traders. The two men have been present since the start of the political meeting, having been notified beforehand by Richard Annenberg, the athletic and sporting outfitter. At his insistence, the suffragette rally has been transformed into an anti-suffragette protest that has spilt from Messina Avenue into the high road. The spillage has not only brought traffic to a standstill, but, inevitably, police reinforcements to the scene. Angry punches are thrown in the ensuing fracas. While women shriek and hemmed-in horses continue to whine and scuffling men fill the air with spittled curses, Jack escorts a grateful employer out of the frenzied maze. During the expedient retreat, Mr Laurence is struck on the head by a blood-stained set of 10/6 teeth. Jack assures him that the blood on his pate is not his own but Mr Laurence is not so certain. Smelling the blood, no doubt, a member of the local press appears on the scene.

"Jenkins. Willesden Chronicle. Can you tell me what happened?"

The bleeding confectioner juts out his chin and straightens his tie. "Well, it was like this, you see. We traders..."

"Can I have the name and number of the shop, as well as your own, please," Jenkins-Willesden-Chronicle interrupts him.

"Certainly: Ernest V. Laurence, that's with a 'u', Confectioner, 221 High Road Kilburn."

"Go on."

"Well, you see, we traders, for a long time now, have been complaining to the authorities about the meetings in Messina Avenue. They're awfully bad for trade."

"How'd you get the cut on your head?"

Mr Laurence glances self-consciously at his employee before replying,

"I was hit by a missile of some sort."

"Much obliged," says the reporter, tapping the brim of his hat with his pencil. As frustrated motorists give vent to their feelings perched atop the roofs of their cars, Jenkins turns and is swallowed up by the crowd.

It is Friday, 18th May, and Mr Laurence is eagerly scanning the columns of the Willesden Chronicle. "Ah! 'Outfitter arrested in anti-suffragist protest...traffic was brought to a complete...Mr Ernest V. Laurence.' Ah!" He points it out to Jack. "There! They've even spelt my name right."

"Wai' till I show Rose!"

"'... bleeding profusely from the head...'"

(Richard Annenberg was fined 20s. and 2s. costs at Maryle-
bone Police Court a month later, and was thereafter regarded
with the utmost respect by his fellow traders and growing clien-
tele.)

There are only forty-eight hours to go, and Jack is still smiling.
Thursday, 22nd June. A king is being crowned in Westminster
Abbey at an estimated cost of £185,000. In the swollen womb of
one of his subjects, a child awaits its own crowning moment (at
an estimated cost of a few pounds) with marked insouciance: the
oversize head that will rival even Humpty's has yet to engage.

Appeased by her knowing midwife and comforting-Corona-
tion-celebrating husband, Rose tries to shrug off her strange
feelings of unease by joining in the cheery street festivities. A
humble feast lies waiting on Union Jack-draped tables. Chairs
and old crates are brought out for the aged and the infirm.
Groups of men drink ale and nudge each other in the ribs while
wives, mothers and mothers-to-be busy themselves gregrariously
under the bunting. The hum of festive activity and the lure of
food soon transform the flag-covered world of the undertables
into a bountiful den for uninvited cats and dogs. The scavengers
are tolerated until, not content with the scraps available, one of
them sinks its teeth into the leg of a child. Horrified adults put
celebratory feelings to one side and set upon the animals with
chairs and crates gallantly vacated by the old and the sick. Cats
prove more elusive targets for a number of reasons: they are far
nimbler than their canine cohorts; they have no fewer than nine
lives, and, what is more, their assailants' swipes are tempered by
the knowledge that the guilty party is not from their ranks. None
of these things can be said of the dogs. They are relatively
awkward and heavy of movement; have a single life to play with,
and the child-biter is among their number. Not surprisingly,
therefore, the majority of them land at least one blow before
scampering to safety. Amid the terrified barking and yelping that
has supplanted the festive hum, three dogs are successfully
cornered and beaten to death.

Perspiring expiators return to the tables in weary triumph,
but few will be so fortunate in the latter half of the decade

following grander exploits. For the moment, though, the chairs and crates are replaced and the ale begins to flow in earnest. The bitten child has been rushed by his parents to the local doctor. Westminster Abbey seems a long way away as the conversation turns to the pressing subject of rabies along the entire length of the train of tables. "Was it froffin' at the mouf?" "Was its tail between its legs?" The consensus of opinion appears to be that, mercifully, the animal was not rabid. "You know wha' children are like wiv dogs." "Probably frigh'ened it." "Pulled its tail." "Stuck a fork in it." "'Appens all the time." Meanwhile, the young victim's friends stare at the three sacrificial carcasses in a semi-circle of fascination and repugnance. The bodies are slumped together like discarded pelts. Open mouths trickle blood on to fur bestrewn with large, black flies. Man's inhumanity to man's best friend – a perverse image of things to come. A broken chair-leg is poked into one of the lifeless abdomens, temporarily disturbing the flies.

Rose clutches her midriff and lets out a sharp cry. By the time Jack has bounded over, the pain of the first contraction has already subsided. Concerned neighbours look on as he carries his wife into the house. From the upstairs window Jack shouts, "Someone ge' Mrs Bowman!"

That June night in 1911 dragged on and on. Drunken choruses of "Long live the King" and other, more obscene proclamations were heard well into the early hours of the 23rd. Arrests were rife. Bands of merry men walked, or rather staggered the streets in open defiance of the Teetotal Crusade and the British Women's Temperance Association. Among those arrested and fined 5/- on that historic night was Jack's old friend, Fred Russell. It had not been Fred's year. A carman by profession, he had already been charged with "cruelty to a horse by working it while lame", and fined 10/- and costs. As if that were not enough to make a man despair, and although it had been on the cards for decades, 1911 was also the year that it finally dawned on the luckless Fred that his fellow citizens really did prefer the spurious horse-power of motor cars and omnibuses to the genuine horse-power that he and other carmen were in the now precarious business of supplying. Unable to rival modern means of transport, flogging a lame horse for a living and flogging a dead one were essentially one and the same thing. It was clearly just a matter of time before twentieth century cities turned their concrete backs for good on the noble beasts that had served them so well for so long. An inebriated, arrested, fined and generally despondent Fred had no way of knowing that the military glory that would lead to his beatification was but a few years away. He was equally oblivious to the fact that while he sat dejectedly in an overcrowded police cell, his friend 'Jacko' was busy complying with a time-honoured tradition.

"Do sit down, Mr Kitchener. We'll wear away the floorboards if we're not careful. There's really nothing to worry about."

"Can I see 'er now?"

Mrs Bowman shuts the bedroom door behind her, and gazes down at her matronly bosom with professional aplomb. "She's fast asleep now. The contractions can't make up their mind whether they're coming or going. I'm afraid there's nothing we can do but wait. I'll be back first thing in the morning. Do try and get some rest, Mr Kitchener."

The heaving breasts are adamant.

Four in the morning. A little over twenty-four hours to go. Mr Kitchener cannot, for the life of him, get some rest because, quite simply, he has no idea what is happening. The bedroom door remains dutifully closed, and the nervous pacing has ceased. He would, however, have continued to cover every inch of the room if he had not been struck by the thought that the twilight-enhanced creaking of the floorboards might disturb his wife. Seated on a chair, elbows on knees, head propped up, the pacing goes on. Is she or isn't she in labour? If the contractions can't make up their mind whether they're coming or going, why has Rose been doubled up by them? Could it mean that the fate that befell her mother... The process of childbirth had always seemed an uncomplicated business to him. How could it seem otherwise to a man whose own mother had given birth no fewer than twelve times in as many years without, to his knowledge, the slightest hint of a complication?

Every now and then a faint moan behind the closed door makes him sit bolt upright. Listening, waiting. But no other sounds are forthcoming, and the concentrated pacing of a troubled mind is resumed...

"Jack."

He flings open the door and rushes to her side. There is a staleness in the air.

"I must've dozed off, luv. You alrigh'? Were you callin' me a long time? I..."

He feels his hand being squeezed in the same measured way it was two years earlier at the rink. "Jack," her tearful eyes, unlike then, are full of foreboding. "I'm scared. I can' 'elp thinkin' abou' me mum..."

Rose buries her head in his arms. Every uncontrollable sob is accompanied by an abrupt rise and fall of the nine-month growth beneath the sheets.

"Firs' one's always the 'ardest, luv. Tha's all."

She plants a gentle kiss on his lips, and wipes away the tears. "Jack, I'm all righ' now. Try and ge' some rest. You look tired."

"You soun' jus' like Mrs Bowman." He smiles, brushing her forelock to one side. "Is it...very painful?"

Stroking the generous curve between them, she lets out a deep, rueful sigh before uttering the "Sometimes" she hopes will not worry him unduly.

The large red clock suspended above the inn informs Friday morning passers-by in High Road Kilburn that it is three minutes past ten. One of them, Miss Dill, is standing directly beneath it, peering up at an embossed lion of matching colour. In her hand is a neatly-cut-out advertisement that reads "Young lady wanted for experiment in telepathy – Apply manager Red Lion Hotel, Kilburn 9." A lad with dark, bag-upholstered eyes, and reeking of nits and vermin pomade, greets Miss Dill with the news that Mr Macaulay, the manager, is momentarily indisposed. Miss Dill agrees to wait inside, unperturbed by the pungent pomade or wafts of stale beer. Red-jacketed gentlemen astride leaping steeds stare down at her from yellowing walls. A servant girl carrying a ewer of water enters the lounge and is taken aback by the sight of the early-morning visitor. Miss Dill pretends not to notice her. The girl winks at the boy, then puts down the ewer with a splash. "Lookin' fer a job?" "She's waitin' t'see the guvnor," explains the lad in a conciliatory tone that betrays his deference to those classed as his 'social betters'. "Beggin' yer pardon," replies the girl, sarcastically. The boy looks half-puzzled, half-apologetic. He is not yet attuned to the justifiably suspicious ways of concubines like the servant girl.

"*So* sorry to keep you waiting," declares Mr Macaulay, entering. He is a burly man prematurely endowed with a middle-age paunch and ruddy complexion.

"I came about the advertisement," Miss Dill informs him, rising to her feet just as he is about to sit down beside her.

"Of course," replies Mr Macaulay, semi-standing, semi-sitting. "The experiment... Would you care for something before we begin?"

The servant girl shakes her head reprovingly, picks up the ewer and shuffles out of the lounge.

"Am I to understand that you will be conducting the experiment yourself? *Here*?"

"Why yes. I'm a great believer in the power of telepathic communication. But we shan't be conducting it here, Miss...?"

"Dill."

"Miss Dill, of course we shan't. These things need to be done properly, so if you'll kindly follow me..."

His motioning arm is pointing invitingly to the door through which the servant girl made her exit. The boy remains motionless, observing the scene with the same puzzled-apologetic expression, as taken for granted by the two protagonists as the proverbial fly on the wall.

"But are you qualified in these matters?" asks Miss Dill, reluctant to accede to his request.

"I believe my experience qualifies me...yes. I'll pay handsomely."

"There is no need for that, I assure you."

"Of course not," he says with an acknowledging glance at her elegant coiffure and dress. The arm still beckons.

The rarefied Hampstead air that Miss Dill has breathed in for the past nineteen years has not prepared her for this. Caught between her instinctive misgivings and her inability to extricate herself graciously from the situation, she begins yielding to the insistent demand of the arm that motions, points, beckons...

"You see...my friends, my family – they don't understand."

Mr Macaulay smiles sympathetically. "People with your...gift find it terribly difficult to be taken seriously. I expect your family think you're...not all there."

"Quite," utters Miss Dill lowering her gaze.

The lounge door opens onto a narrow, dilapidated hall reeking of uric acid. A flight of rickety stairs takes the manager of the Red Lion Hotel and his telepathic companion to the former's private quarters. Mr Macaulay claims that his lack of relevant qualifications notwithstanding he is preparing a paper on the subject of inter-mental communication that will rock the foundations of the scientific world. Miss Dill conceals her surprise as she stares at the roughly-made bed which dominates the small room. Overbearing beams run across a sagging ceiling. Mr Macaulay places two chairs in the middle of the room, and invites Miss Dill to sit in one of them. To promote good results, he draws the curtains before sitting down opposite her.

"If you'd care to shut your eyes, Miss Dill, we'll commence."

"Won't you be annotating?"

"Keep it all up here," he says, touching his brow. "I'll write it up later."

"I see," remarks Miss Dill, who, against her better judgement; in spite of the pomade and the beer and the uric acid; spurred by the prospect of finally being able to share her unusual talent with someone who appears to be interested and willing to cooperate, cannot help but look forward with relish to the experiment she is on the verge of taking part in.

"Now, when you're ready – that's right, close your eyes – I'll start thinking of an object and try projecting it to you. Don't worry if we don't get any results at first. Our minds have to...get to know each other first."

Under the beams, in the middle of a dark, bed-dominated room, treated every now and then to the distant singing of a scrubbing concubine, two alien minds are attempting against all the odds to establish ground-breaking contact.

"Picking up anything?" whispers the aficionado projector of mental images.

The intended receiver replies with a deliberate nod of the head. With a separate gesture of the hand, which, given its silken texture, glows even in the prevailing gloom, she indicates that he must be patient a little longer. Failing to control the deep feelings of excitement triggered by her positive response, Mr Macaulay draws his chair fractionally closer. Minutes later, Miss Dill opens her eyes.

"I got something..."

"Excellent!"

"Only the strange thing is I don't think I was receiving it from you."

The darkness; the close proximity in which they find themselves obliges them to speak in hushed, almost intimate tones.

"The first image I got was...well, it kept changing from what seemed to me to be some sort of gun – the barrel, you understand – to a clenched fist with the index finger prominent."

"Really?"

"Yes – first the barrel, then the finger..."

"Did it...change into any other object?"

She is concentrating too hard to detect the change in Mr Macaulay's voice. "No. After that I..." His right knee has entered into gloom-assisted contact with her left. "I..." nervously clearing her throat as a warm glow radiates through the fabric of her skirt; "I received the vision," dismissing the foolish notion that they are not alone, "of a room not unlike this one. A woman was crying out a man's name...Jack, I think it was."

"Well, all I can say is that you were very warm with the first one...very warm indeed. Shall we try again?"

Eyes tightly shut, the experiment is resumed. Slowly but surely, Miss Dill overcomes her innermost apprehensions, and aided, rather than hampered, by the atonal cantatrice downstairs, she finally manages to tune into the mind of her co-experimenter. Yes, there he is: surrounded by a group of men and walls bearing familiar paintings of immaculate huntsmen on their mounts. All the men are holding tankards. Suddenly, a guffaw explodes like a cannon-shot. A newspaper is produced; passed around. One man shouts, "Jim'll do anyfink to win a wager!" Another is convinced that "no one'd be so stupid as t'bite *tha'* bait." "Just wait and see," a confident Mr Macaulay tells them. The vision fades and is instantly replaced by... "No!" A chair crashes noisily to the ground as Miss Dill rushes across the room and draws back the curtains. Blinded by the light, Mr Macaulay fumbles awkwardly around the area of his groin. Miss Dill suppresses a shriek and, in averting her gaze from the now familiar but no less offensive protrusion, she rests it, alas, on a collection of red-faced men of varying age huddling in a corner of the room. A nauseous Miss Dill scampers to the door, down the rickety stairs, through the malodorous hall, past the leaping steeds, and concubine, and young lad, and into the relative sanity of the high road.

The large red clock suspended overhead informs Friday afternoon passers-by in Kilburn that it is fast approaching a quarter past twelve.

Mrs Bowman is as good as her word, seven thirty qualifying in even the most ardent of early risers' book as "first thing in the morning". To her chagrin, she finds Rose up and about in the tiny kitchen-dining-living room.

"Mrs Kitchener! What do we think we're doing?"

"I'm makin' us a cuppa tea. I'm so tired of lyin' down."

"Couldn' stop 'er," says Jack rather guiltily.

"But what of our contractions?" she persists, not taking any notice of him. The pointed, heaving cushions are not amused.

"They stopped a few hours ago. I don' think there's any..."

"Well if you want my advice, Mrs Kitchener, it's straight back to bed with you."

"Oh, do I have to?"

"We're certainly in no condition to be making cups of tea."

"Come on, luv, you better do as you're told. I'll brin' yer the tea."

"That's more like it," pronounces a satisfied Mrs Bowman as she leads her charge into the bedroom.

When a tea-laden Jack tries entering the room, his entry is barred by an advancing, hand-raising, breast-buffeted matron who informs him that she is about to conduct an internal examination. Jack utters "Oh", hands her the tray and is about to close the door when she adds, "We *are* going to work today, aren't we?"

Jack shakes his head timidly. "I got word to Mr Laurence las' nigh' an' 'e said I needn'..."

"Come now! I always encourage my husbands to carry on as normal. What possible good can you do here?"

Jack peers forlornly into the room, but Rose is eclipsed by a matronly shoulder. "I suppose yer righ'," he hears himself mutter.

So, thus despatched, an understandably confused father-to-be makes his way to number 221 High Road Kilburn, where his equally confused employer greets him with, "What the devil do you think you're doing here?"

Elisabeth Kitchener is what is absurdly known as a general. The only men under her command are incontinent little boys whom, even more absurdly, she is required to address as 'master'. Her superiors are the Marshalls, but not, as one would expect, field-marshalls. She is, of course, a general servant: a domestic.

At twenty, she is a year younger than Jack, which means she is the second oldest of the Kitchener brood. She lives and works in a large house in Kensal Rise, and, following in her mother's footsteps, attends the College for Working Women in Fitzroy Street every weekday evening. Elisabeth, who will be known as aunt Libby to her 'son', is a restrained supporter of the suffragette movement, and an inveterate lover of English literature. She has written a letter to the Misses Nickels, the respected principals of the Cricklewood and Willesden Green High School and Kindergarten, "humbly offering my services in the field of literary instruction". Much to her delight, the missive was well-received. "We would be only too happy to consider your kind application to join our staff if and when the opportunity arises." Garlanded with a blue ribbon, the encouraging reply is as cherished as the voluminous correspondence of her suitors: not mere mortals these, but the consecrated likes of Shakespeare, Marlowe, Pope, Keats, Tennyson, Byron, Wordsworth, Shelley ...their every inspired word penned with her, and her alone, in mind.

With the time fast approaching a quarter past twelve under a large red clock in the high road, Elisabeth lets out a startled cry as she is almost knocked to the ground by a young lady in a desperate hurry. Catching her breath, she stares curiously at the fleeing figure and at the inn door from which she charged like a frightened animal. Ten minutes later, nursing a slightly bruised forearm, Elisabeth turns right into an Eresby Road that smells of dead dog. No swift-footed messenger has summoned her to the side of her brother and parturient sister-in-law. She has come of her own accord, sensing, quite inexplicably, that she is needed. So strong was her intuition that she had no hesitation at all in requesting permission from her understanding employers to pay an emergency visit. However, it was beyond her unsuspected powers of apprehension that she would not be returning to active service in the Marshall household.

The anguished cry she hears coming from the upstairs window as she is about to knock on the door provides instant confirmation of her intuited concern.

"You must be Mrs Bowman," deduces Elisabeth, contemplating the perspiring obstetrician who has just opened the door. "I'm Jack's sister." And quick to register that the corpulent figure standing before her does not adopt the genialness of manner that a persona grata rightly expects, she adds, "I've come to see Rose."

"I'm afraid," asseverates the obdurate concierge, "that you couldn't have chosen a worse time to visit Mrs Kitchener. She's just gone into labour."

"On the contrary, I don't believe I could have timed my visit any better. Now, if you'll excuse me," squeezing past the disdainfully heaving, positively rancorous breasts, and ascending the stairway with quiet determination. Rose's face lights up the moment her husband's sister steps into the room.

"Lisabeth, I'm so glad you've come!"

Drawing on the cumulative wealth of experience so generously bequeathed to her by many of her suitors' dramatis personae, Elisabeth is able to conceal the terrible shock produced in her by the sight of a sickly pale and haggard Rose. The folds of her nightclothes, like the hair upon her brow, are thickly plaited with sweat; ominous rings encircle weary eyes, their bluey-blackness enhanced by ashen cheeks.

"I thought the baby wasn't due until next week," she remarks jovially, kneeling beside the bed.

A dark shadow is cast by Mrs Bowman's hefty frame in the doorway.

"Tha' wha' *I* though'," replies Rose, managing a smile that is all gratitude as she takes Elisabeth's hand in hers. "I'm so glad you've come!"

"As you can see for yourself, Miss Kitchener, she needs to rest."

"Tell me exactly what it feels like," urges Elisabeth with infectious enthusiasm.

The unheeded shadow shifts with professional unease.

"It's the strangest thing... One minute it feels as (*pausing for breath*) the pain'll never go away. Then (*pausing*) it goes away, and it doesn' come back for ages. It's as if they can' make up their minds (*glancing at Mrs Bowman*). It's been worse since Jack left. I've (*pausing*) been callin' ou' 'is name all day. At this rate (*smiling tiredly, pausing yet again for breath*) it *will* be born nex' week."

"In that case, how would you like it if I washed you down and changed the bedclothes? I'm sure you'd feel more comfortable."

The grateful grip is tightened. "But promise me tha' when you've done tha' you'll fetch Jack."

"Mrs Kitchener..."

"Of course I'll fetch him, Rose," interrupts Elisabeth with a tone of such gentle finality that even Mrs Bowman is forced to surrender to her unsolicited consent.

One hour later, refreshed and cheek-pinched, Rose welcomes back her husband with trembling, open arms. In the adjoining room, Mrs Bowman informs Miss Kitchener that, in view of the lethargic nature of the confinement, her continued presence is not strictly necessary, and that she will therefore be returning home for a late afternoon repast.

And gradually, as imperceptibly at first as the revolving hands of a clock, the frequency of the contractions increases. Unshackled from her bed, Rose finds that the painful waves begin to arrive more quickly but are of a much shorter duration. Despite this, perhaps through sheer exhaustion or on the grounds of impropriety (that it would somehow be unseemly to give in to the natural desire she feels to squat), she eventually decides to reassume the orthodox recumbent position, whereupon the contractions become markedly more sluggish.

Jack and Elisabeth are constantly by her side, uttering words of comfort; patiently stroking the intumescent abdomen when it seems the pain will never, ever subside. They conjure up endless flannels with which to soak up the sweat that oozes from her brow and from the cheeks that have long since lost their colour.

Every now and then, Jack is obliged to lean out of the window to satiate the good-hearted curiosity of his neighbours.

When Mrs Bowman returns in the early evening, her matronly bosom is still prominent but no longer intimidating. The rate of cervical dilation is found to be as lethargic and as sluggish as the rate of the contractions. This is still so when, late into the candlelit evening of that post-Coronation, pre-crowning Friday, Mrs Bowman elects to administer the push she thinks the labour needs to start it rolling: rupturing the mother's waters. From this point on, and for the next twelve, eternal hours, the cranked-up pangs of childbirth grow more and more unbearable. Chrysalid minutes hatch agonisingly into quarters of hours...half hours... hours... At midnight, the 23rd of June becomes the 24th...one in the morning becomes two...three...four...as screams succeed screams, pain succeeds pain... How much longer? The question is on all lips save the bloodless ones of Rose, for whom time has frozen in a mesmerizing alternation of respite and torture. Beginning to sense the worst, Jack and his sister silently beseech God to show mercy and intervene. There is nothing like raw suffering and crippling fear to transmute the faith of the believer into a desperate hope that the Creator of all things does indeed possess an infinite capacity for compassion; that divine help comes, bidden or unbidden, to those who are deserving.

The light streaming into the bedroom is already strong and golden when Mrs Bowman suddenly shouts, "Push!" The command is repeated over and over again. "Push!" It is a tripartite command, for Jack and Elisabeth have re-invested all their faith and hopes into this one cry: "Push!" The English language has been reduced to a single word – no other will do, and it is uttered with the monotonous regularity of an incantation. Push! Push! Push! When Rose fails to respond, the obsessive chants are intensified. PUSH PUSH PUSH

Her knees forming an oblique, blood-stained V; her head hung back to expose the tautest of muscular reliefs, the mother-to-be cries and screams and yells, but does not, cannot PUSH. In a desperate attempt to make her do so, fraternal arms are interlocked to prop her up so that matronly hands clamped around her legs can press counter-resistively forward. The Victorian,

Edwardian and newly-instigated Georgian sense of propriety having been well and truly drowned in a raging sea of blood and sweat, the eyes of the chanting trio are now unabashfully trained on an area of pubescence dilated with imminent eruption. But the progenital lava refuses to flow.

A glinting, pincerlike instrument is uncased. Last resort. Nothing else we can do. She's got nothing left to push with. Grave, corroborative looks. Carefully, methodically, the device is inserted into the plethoric entrance, occasioning the smallest of tears on one side. Submerged in her tormented, timeless world, Rose, her eyes shut; her countenance a harrowed mass of lines, barely seems to register the intrusive presence or the wound that it unwittingly inflicts. Finding it increasingly difficult to reconcile the squirming woman in front of him with his Rose, Jack turns his back on the proceedings. Leaving Mrs Bowman to her thankless, gory task, Elisabeth redirects her boundless reserves of sympathy to her distraught brother.

The forceps are in position. Tentatively, with the concentration it would require to secure an egg in the iron jaws of a vice without cracking it, the pressure is applied. And slowly... cautiously...the bloody wrench is withdrawn, but when a tender crown makes contact with the mouth of the torn vulva, Rose emerges from the spellbinding depths of her ordeal with an excruciating cry. Jack and Elisabeth spin around with a start. Unable to accommodate the largest part of the baby's head and the extra width of the forceps, they are forced to hold her down while, at this vital moment (no moment can be *more* vital), the acutest of pains flows through her like an electric current. Almost ...nearly there...coming...

New screams fill the birth-soiled room. "It's a boy!" announces Mrs Bowman, cradling the infant. Rose collapses limply into her husband's arms, free at long last of the cruel voltage.

"He's a big'un, Jack. No wonder he wouldn't come out!" exclaims a jubilant Elisabeth.

Jack nods wearily. "Eyes shu' jus' like a kit'en's. Bless 'im!"

"The cord was round his neck," says the midwife, reaching for some scissors. "When I've seen to the cord I'll tend to Mrs Kitchener's bleeding."

While Mrs Bowman attempts to stem the steady flow of blood,

and Elisabeth holds her nephew, Jack stares into his wife's eyes with an odd, reciprocated mixture of unending devotion and sad resignation. There is an unmistakable air of homecoming and departure.

"You got yer boy, Jack." Her voice is a whisper. "Le' me 'old 'im."

Elisabeth hands her the baby with such care and concern that it is obvious to everyone that she doubts Rose has the strength to hold him.

"Rose...I'm so proud of yer, luv," says Jack, placing his arms around the two of them."

"Take good care of 'im, Jack."

"Wha' kiner talk's tha'?" he mockingly rebukes her.

But the eyes cannot conceal the pressing truth: instead of Rose's cheeks, it is the lower half of the sheets that are losing their pallor.

"Lisabeth's such an angel... If anythin'..."

"Rose, please... Don' waste your breath. You look so tired, luv."

A tear rolls down bone-white cheeks. Jack wipes it gently away.

"Jack," her voice is now a faint echo as she holds the baby as tightly as she can, "if 'e cries at nigh' make sure you use a soother with one of those respiration shields. I think Spence's..."

"Don' worry about tha' now, luv... We'll 'ave plen'y of time ter..."

Her head slumps onto his arm. "Rose! Rose!" Two eyes take him in with an impassive serenity – two mirrors reflecting an irrevocable expression of grief. "Rose!"

Rosalind Anne Kitchener was laid to rest in Fortune Green Cemetery beside her mother Mary. Her ailing father, George, as he had done eighteen years earlier, and perhaps sensing that he would soon be joining his loved ones, threw down the first handful of earth with the deep consternation of a broken man. Behind him, another broken man, flanked on one side by a caring employer, and on the other by an infant-cradling sister, was tearfully and imperceptibly beating out a tattoo in time to the once rousing music of a certain Professor Voorzanger and his band.

Two

Historical events, which all too often involve protracted warfare and carnage, are traditionally recorded for posterity in a way that suggests that life is a temporal chessboard on which the 'historic' moves of 'historic' individuals or regimes can be neatly broken down and analysed, not to mention their impact on the 'masses'. On such a chessboard, the suffering and death of an historically insignificant person like Rose Kitchener would figure no more prominently than an infinitesimal part of a tiny speck of dust on an actual chessboard (some would argue that the ratio is a flattering one). However, it would be impossible for anyone to deny that even an infinitesimal part of a tiny speck of dust has a justifiable claim to microcosmic relevance. The nine-month cycle that ended tragically with a bloody giving and taking of life was a reflection of an historical sequence of not always deliberate moves destined to result in one of the goriest, flesh-rending sacrifices of willing and conscripted pawns ever witnessed by other pawns, knights, bishops, and kings. Who initiated this baneful cycle? Who executed the first of numerous complex and deadly moves? An accusing finger as erect with righteousness as one that would send so many to their deaths is pointing frantically to a biblical passage detailing Man's Fall from Grace (it is a clerical digit that naturally concerns itself with fundamental moral causes rather than transient effects). Not to be outdone, a lay finger taps authoritatively on a glossy textbook theorising prosaically on the origin of life in the cosmic wilderness – from which every resulting effect can *really* be traced. Tut-tutting, and with a shake of the head, the learned historian draws everyone's attention back to the board in question and singles out one of the major pieces at the heart of *this* particular event: Wilhelm or William II, the German Emperor. And it should, of course, surprise none of us, for if an infinitesimal part of a tiny speck of dust was capable of entertaining dreams of gas cookers, high street sales, and a particular brand of dummy, then a towering piece like the Kaiser could, without batting a Teutonic eyelid, entertain dreams of supreme world domination. Willingly influenced by only-by-war-can-Germany-achieve-the-supremacy-nature-intended-for-her philosophising philosophers like Heinrich von Treitschke, the cycle was initiated; the first fatal moves executed...the impregnating seed sown. Thereafter, a fertilised Europe, freshly produced by the ovary of the twentieth century, split into two when, on one side, Austria-Hungary, Germany and Italy, and, on the other, France, Russia and Great Britain established their respective Triple Alliance and Triple Entente. It was now only a matter of time. Pacifists and optimists alike prayed daily for a war-averting miscarriage, while the realists and the pessimists, well aware that the embryo was being superbly nourished, speculated on the likeliest dates that an overflying stork disguised as an airship would appear over their rooftops. Growing (crisis in Morocco). Getting bigger (Bosnian crisis). Swelling (Balkan wars). Push! (Sarajevo murders). And what would this world-shattering foetus be called? The Great War, of course (later renamed, in modern cinematographic vein, World War I, to avoid confusing it with its sequel, the 1939-45 epic production: World War II. The name by which it will be known in its next incarnation is thus depressingly predictable, as is the regional matrix from which it will issue).

However, as has long been the case and will continue to be so, it falls to the weaver of fictions to approach the board in question and run a Sistine-like forefinger over the black and white squares and the tabulated version of History they so aptly represent. And as it skirts carefully around the regal and aristocratic pieces, it begins to gather up a thickening film of dust-particles hitherto invisible to the scholastic eye. Gradually, the greyish mass dragged this way and that through the historical macrocosm acquires faint, ever-lengthening strands that fan out behind it like the swirling tail of a comet – that mythological bearer of life...

There were pressing questions to be answered, and none more so than "Who's going to look after the baby?" One grand-mother was dead, the other, run off her feet looking after her own children. As was natural in one so noble of character, though, Lady, as she was affectionately known by the family, offered to raise her first grandson herself. One mouth more to feed; one mouth less... Elisabeth would have none of it. She was clearly destined to this form of immaculately-conceived mother-hood. The uncanny way that she had felt the need to visit Rose; her part in reuniting her with Jack so that they could be together for the final hours; the way she was on hand to take care of the child when tragedy struck; what Rose had said about her...all these factors indicated that she was poetically justified in con-sidering herself the natural choice. Frank Kitchener, a strong, burly man forever smelling of freshly-sawn timber, and someone who was inclined to regard the poetically justifiable as "a load of ol' rubbish", took his daughter to one side on the morning of Rose's funeral and posed her the following question,

"Wha'll become of all yer books an' all yer teachin'?"

"I've given it a lot of thought, Dad, I really have. It's like a calling...a vocation. I just know I have to do it."

Calloused carpenter's hands gesture beseechingly. "Bu' won-cha regre' it, pet? Yer young. You could 'ave a change of 'eart."

"But don't you see? I *won't* be giving up teaching. All my studies won't be wasted – little Frankie shall be my one and only pupil. I can teach *him*...Dad, I know it's what Rose wanted."

And so it was. A small case (containing, among other personal effects, a blue-garlanded letter) and a pile of impressive-looking books were transported from Kensal Rise to Kilburn in Fred Russell's horse-drawn car. Unimaginably, a general had become a mother.

Jack remained on the fringes of his family's crucial delibera-tions. He was as shell-shocked as if the Kaiser's stork had decided to deliver its mortiferous cargo prematurely. Off work (Mr Laurence had immediately insisted that he take a couple of weeks' paid leave), he would sit for hours, staring blankly at the wall. Transfixed, in an emotional form of suspended animation, hardly any food or water passed his lips. He refrained from shaving.

Harshly-drawn curtains veiled the outside world. Concerned knocks on doors went unanswered. Stale air grew staler.

Occasionally, falling prey to the cruel tricks of synaesthesia, a floorboard creaking with disturbing familiarity brings Jack violently to his senses. Turning, hoping against hope, searching ...a flower's name on his lips. There are two pools of love-stained glass. And cold, ashen cheeks. And... What's that glinting menacingly in the corner? A woman's voice fills the room. No, it's the mellow tones of Rev. Richards. "Jack." Halitosis. Jonquil teeth. "What the Lord giveth, the Lord..."

"Jack!"

Blinding light. Sheltered eyes make out a bodiced silhouette. "Rose?" Tentative steps forward. Arms outstretched.

"Jack, it's me – Elisabeth."

Such an angel. If anything...

"Elisabeth?"

Someone laden with books and a case in the hazy background, who addresses him as 'Jacko', takes his leave of the Kitcheners.

Hauled into the real world by a sister with a proverbial old head on young shoulders, Jack played his resigned part in converting the matrimonial bedroom into Elisabeth and Frankie's room. Linen was boiled and aired; drawers re-lined; shelves dusted; books stacked. However, an imposing wardrobe housing the bulk of Rose's clothes was left respectfully untouched. This was Elisabeth's sole concession to her bereaved brother's deep-seated moroseness. Though much averse to sharing her new room with what amounted to a mausoleum, such wishes, she felt, had to be tolerated. The modest transformation was completed with the addition of a sturdy cradle designed and assembled by Frank Kitchener to mark the birth of his first grandchild.

Out of sheer necessity, the kitchen-dining-living room had also to quadruple as Jack's 'bedroom'. Every evening, two thick woollen blankets were placed on the floor, one on top of the other, to form a makeshift mattress, and every morning the cumbersome pair were folded up and put away. Still reeling from the mighty blow life had dealt him, steeped in the melancholic incredulity of someone who expects to wake up at any moment from a terrifying nightmare, Jack attached little importance to such relatively insignificant hardship. He even acquiesced to the culinary preferences of a visiting rat one night by dreamily allowing it to nibble his uncovered toe. A horrified Elisabeth, alerted the next morning by the sight of bloodstains on his sheet, wasted no time in entreating her father to devise a collapsable bed that would be inconspicuous by day and rat-safe by night. The response was immediate. While Jack rocked the baby's cradle with his bandaged foot in one room, the master carpenter hammered and sawed in the other, waited on by his grateful daughter. Several hours later, a 6' x 3' length of timber hung from the wall on six strong hinges. Smaller hinges on the reverse side allowed the all-important supports to fold away horizontally. Elisabeth was delighted, and she was even more delighted when her father offered to cover the larger cracks in the floor and skirting with his off-cuts.

One Sunday, the day before Jack's official period of mourning was due to end (it was back to work on the Monday), the cast expression of profound, incurable grief buckled into the hint of a smile. This major psychological breakthrough occurred while the cherubic buttocks of Frank Laurence Kitchener were being meticulously swabbed by his aunt. The truth of the matter was that little Frankie had not been a pretty sight. All new arrivals, of course, greet the breath-bated world with toothless, mangled faces. Deformed heads with constricted brows are not uncommon. Unfortunately, when forceps are deployed, bruised, deformed heads and constricted brows are the sorry order of the day. Young Kitchener was no exception. His squashed features and rugby-ball head would have seemed uncompromisingly offensive to most self-respecting fathers, let alone one whose wife had died shortly after giving birth to him. But time, as they say, is a good healer. As Jack watched his sister at work on that bottom-swabbing Sunday afternoon, it suddenly dawned on him that his son's face and head looked decidedly normal. A closer examination bore out that the puffy, boxer's features and ovoid cranium were no more. But something else had changed too. With that first hint of a smile, Jack cried, " 'Is eyes! Sis, 'is eyes...they're Rose's!"

For the first time since moving in, Elisabeth was able to breathe a little easier.

It is becoming considerably treacherous underfoot on the historian's chessboard. Italian, Serbian, Greek, Bulgarian, and, above all, Turkish blood is flowing freely across it. After seizing the Turkish province of Tripoli (King's Knight to Bishop 2), the Italians have declared war on Turkey. There is more. While thus engaged, a newly-formed 'Balkan League' has ganged up on the Turks, inflicting a crushing defeat. The Gregorian Calendar has flicked its way to 1913, and the Germans and Austrians are as amused by all of this as a famous monarch of old or the historically-overlooked bust of Mrs Bowman at her gravest.

English blood is also being spilt, though not in such large quantities or, as yet, on the board itself. The Commissioner of Police for the City of London is as amused as the Germans and the Austrians. There is no doubt about it: the fault lies squarely with the pedestrians. Their careless behaviour on the increasingly busy roads and thoroughfares of the metropolis is clearly responsible for the alarming rate of accidents and deaths involving motor-powered vehicles. Much concerned about the welfare of its passengers, and in a welcomed, supportive response to the Commissioner's reprobation, the London General Omnibus Co. Ltd is to issue pictorial announcements showing how to get on and off their motor buses. These, alas, will be of little help to travellers such as George Langdon, who was crushed to death when he alighted from one bus into the reversing path of another inside the Willesden Omnibus Terminal. Witnesses agreed unanimously that Rose's father acted carelessly and had only himself to blame. A passer-by remarked, "Poor bloke didn' know wha' 'it 'im."

A finger limp with piety slowly describes the four points of the Cross. Black umbrellas sheltering mourners in black. A black hole in the black, moist earth. A grey blanket of drizzle conferring upon the nigrescent scene the peculiar charm of a mottled daguerreotype.

The same cannot be said of the hastily-dug graves that lie unattended under the glare of the Turkish sun.

A striking sight: two large towers crowned with coppered domes; a plastered facade with splendidly soft, overlapping cornices; richly ornate doors leading into an impressive vestibule, its marble floor a polished echo of admiring gasps. Inside, no fewer than fifteen hundred patrons are guaranteed a comfortable stay (expertly-sprung seats; concealed lighting) and insuperable visual access (sloping floor; no columns on the balcony). The focal centre of attention, literally, measuring a staggering 20' x 15', will be the recipient of images projected by the most up-to-date and complete bioscope machines on the market. The programme will be changed at least twice-weekly (depending on availability). Aural delights are supplied by a magnificent Mustel Celesta organ and by a superb grand Wagner model Ibach pianoforte. All this and much, much more (including the ladies' favourite: the tea room) at the newly erected Maida Vale Picture Palace. Stalls: 6d and 1/-.

Yes, Frank L. Kitchener was growing up in a very unusual world. Competitors in the European heats of the armament race were sprinting at breakneck speeds. The continent had become a veritable powder-magazine. People were taking to the air in monoplanes and biplanes, and to the roads in motor cars. Palaces were being erected with renascent zeal for the benefit of commoners, while the House of Lords, that age-old bastion of moral and judicial integrity, was having its powers severely curbed by the Liberals. And as if all this were not sufficiently odd and disorientating, women were fastening themselves to official buildings like limpets. Colonies were becoming self-governing dominions. Not least of all, curious umbrella-shaped machines called 'gramophones' were magically filling the air with catchy ditties.

Frankie was not the only one, of course. Shortly after losing a grandfather, he gained a cousin and a new aunt. His uncle Edward (third in line to the family throne, and a labourer by profession) had married Louisa, his lifelong flame, and fathered a baby girl named Charlotte. Although the two infants were not quite yet on speaking terms, it was obvious to everyone that they held each other in high esteem.

Elisabeth and Louisa took to one another with renewed affection, arranging frequent visits to Kilburn Grange Park. Their disparate forms of motherhood had transformed a long-standing acquaintance into an intimate friendship. Starved of a communicative companion, Elisabeth spent as much time as she could with her sister-in-law (despite genuine efforts to put the past behind him, Jack continued to be plagued by bouts of depression, and had never, at the best of times, been a great talker). A steady traffic of confidences flowed between them. Elisabeth's preoccupations centred, invariably, on (a) Jack's state of mind; (b) Frankie's progress (fed on a diet of Neave's Baby Food he was the personification of bonniness), and (c) the merits of the poem, play or novel that she happened to be in the middle of reading. Hers were serious, considered confidences, delivered with an air of frankness that might have been mistaken for naivety. In contrast, and herein lay the mutual attraction, Louisa unburdened her heart with endearing effervescence. States of mind, paediatric development, and the virtues of literature came a very long way behind the subject of sex. Amid hushed giggles; under swaying bowers, while partaking of tea and scones in a palatial tea room...sexual matters surfaced into her conversation like bubbles in a glass of beer. She made no apology for this, especially as she would never have been so coarse as to be explicit. Louisa was a natural exponent of the suggestive art of double entendre, an uncrowned queen of innuendo. At first, Elisabeth had pretended that the covert indecencies were beyond her, but in time, realising that it was a harmless quirk of an otherwise sound character, she began to acknowledge them with a benign, reproving smile. Even though she was uncomfortably junior whenever the mysteries of marriage and relationships came up, and since she was no longer preoccupied with the concerns of almost nineteen months ago, these rose to the top of her table of priorities. Let us consider, for example, the following extract from Elisabeth's diary (entered 15th February 1913):

"What a delightful actress Sarah Bernhardt is. Louisa insisted we go and see her, sweeping aside my financial considerations. And how right she was! 'An Actress's Romance' is a photoplay charged with all the fire and passion of a classic drama. How lucky we were that Lottie remained asleep throughout. I tremble at the thought of what might have happened if the little angel had awakened and, startled by the music and the dark, had started crying. Frankie slept for long periods, sucking ever so vigorously on his soother. I know I would not have taken such a gamble on my own. The idea of perhaps frightening Frankie and marring the enjoyment of others, as well as my own, would surely have held me back. But there seems to be no holding back Louisa. She acts on sudden impulses, and whether the carrying out of these impulses proves beneficial or detrimental to the rest of us is not, I fear, a pertinent consideration on her part. I do not intend this as an uncharitable criticism, but as an earnest observation. I must confess that it is not without a certain amount of envy that I make it. Of late I have been struck by the nature of my own behaviour. I know there is nothing worse, weaker or more un-Christian than to indulge in oneself but I have nevertheless succumbed to the temptation of comparing myself with her. I am not motivated by vanity, or at least I honestly do not think I am. It is not her softness and pallor of skin, or the lightness of her step that I have grown envious of (oh, how it pains me to admit it!) Quite simply, it is that she is married and I am not. This is not to say that I regret the decision I took when dear Rose passed away. No, I shall never regret that as long as I live. Yet I cannot deny that Louisa has opened up an unspeakable curiosity in me for all matters related to affairs of the heart. On each occasion Miss Bernhardt moved to within inches of her leading man, I felt a warm glow of excitement. An effect quite different to any other I have ever experienced while reading about such happenings. Feelings have been stirred in me that I, more so than any other person, know must be controlled. It would be out of the question for me to... No, I dare not even think of it. But what of poor Jack! If a mare can have such desires, then what of the stallion?

"How glad I am that I have at last allowed my innermost thoughts on the matter to find expression on these pages. For this alone, I feel eternally indebted to Louisa."

At the age of twenty-one, Elisabeth had been forced to acknowledge the existence of not only Louisa's sexual innuendoes, but the uncharted world of emotions these betrayed. But the difficulties were there for all to see. What would become of Frankie if she did decide to go in search of that emotional world? Even, but this is pure fantasy...just supposing I, and that the other person agreed to...marry me on the condition that – otherwise there would be no marriage – Frankie remained under my care and tuition... But no! How can I even contemplate it!

Jack's his father. He couldn't possibly have two. Yet what if Jack, and who could blame him? a man's needs are...then *I* would be expected to... No, I couldn't give up Frankie.

Edward, his lifelong flame and the 'delightful', far-famed Sarah Bernhardt had innocently conspired to stir up a hornet's nest. Mr Laurence, of all people, would shortly complete the cocktail of metaphors by dropping a veritable bombshell.

Can an island sink? Is it possible for an enormous landmass to be swallowed up by an ocean's frothing mouth like a truncated liner? Why, then, the nervous, thorny scampering up and down the nation's decks? Why the rat-like desertion to far-flung dominions? Can the fact that the Kitchener household has become a rodent-free haven be solely attributable to a senior craftman's expert nailing? Why are people casting off from Albion's shores in numbers rivalling those that will perish for King and Country in the course of the Great War? Surely this unprecedented exodus cannot be explained away, as some cynics have sought to do, by the suggestion that it is some kind of patriotic reaction to the arrival in Britain of American dances like the Boston, the Turkey trot, and the Bunny Hug. Equally bogus is the claim that there is a direct correlation between an increase in the rate of emigration in 1909 and the grand opening of Selfridges, which introduced an unsuspecting public to soda-fountains and lift-girls in garish costumes.

Leaden clouds with ominously sagging bellies. Clusters of hand-pocketed, foot-stamping men gathered outside an official building. Each gust of wind seems to bring more men. For the sake of solidarity or, perhaps, to generate more warmth, the swelling clusters merge into a single body. Alarmed faces peer at the huddled mass through watery holes of condensation. The first drops begin to fall, but the spirits of a hundred and fifty jobless men remain undampened. Paradoxically, the light drizzle fires their collective resolve. The pungent odour of coats and cloth-caps dripping with rain assumes the invigorating property of smelling-salts. Placards and banners, not umbrellas, are suddenly produced out of thin air. "No, no, no to *daily signing on!*" chant the men as one. A deafening thunderclap confirms that the gods are pleased. More rain to fuel the flames. Harder; harder. "No, no, no to *daily signing on!*" Sodden shoes and boots have disappeared in a fountaineous haze, and the faces behind the glass have ceased to betray alarm. What the wind giveth, the wind and rain taketh away. The unified body is (slowly, very slowly) disbanding. Those on the fringes of the crowd are being swept away like autumn leaves. Soon, only a tiny nucleus of determined protestors stand their ground. "No, no, no to *daily signing on!*" Official windows are allowed to mist up. The remaining men pose all the threat of a hardy band of carol singers.

Abandoned banners. Cursive rivers of red ink. The fantastic calligraphy of the wind.

"These Liberals'll be the death of me, what with Taffy's Insurance Act and whatnot. It's put a few coppers on everything. Why only the other day, Dickie Annenberg was telling me it was all he could do to keep his prices steady for a week at a time. Anyway, we're stuck with them and that's that... Heard the news about Captain Scott, Jack?"

"No."

"He's dead."

"Dead!"

"Frozen stiff."

"Poor bloke."

"Didn't even have the satisfaction of getting to the pole before whatsisname, you know...Amundsen."

"To go all tha' way for nothin'... Don' see the poin', meself."

"We've always been a nation of explorers, Jack. Always will be. It's in our blood, you see, being an island and all that... Drake, Cook, Livingstone, whatsisname – you know, discovered the source of the Nile..."

"Sis would know. I..."

"Speke! Captain John Speke. I knew it was there somewhere."

"All the same, I'd much sooner stay on dry lan' than..."

"No spirit of adventure, that's your trouble, Jack. Why, I'll wager you've never even set foot on the Heath."

"'Course I 'ave. Me an' Ro... I've been there plen'y of times."

"I'm sorry, Jack, I didn't mean to...stir up old memories."

"Tha's all righ'. So 'appens me an' Sis are goin' up there on Sundee. Takin' Frankie."

"How *is* the little devil?"

"I don' know wha' Sis gives 'im, but 'e gets bigger by the day."

"Good. That's what I want to hear... And how's Elisabeth?"

"Oh, I reckon she's all righ'. 'Ard to tell, really. She never complains."

"She's a fine woman, your sister...a fine woman. Earnt her place in God's heaven, have no fear of that. Do anything for her, I would... Yes... Er, Jack, I've been meaning to – I hope you don't mind me asking, but, well, you know, it's been some time since...it all happened, and..."

There is undulating grassland as far as the eye can see.

"He said *what?*"

Under winter-crisp, soot-free skies, the aspiring middle classes amble. Erstwhile riders that they are, their preambulatory progress from hillock to hillock is executed with sublime, equinal grace. Not everyone, it has to be said, has been blessed with the measured elegance of the horse. Courting couples and families move unrhythmically among them. Ever since the ill-judged opening of Hampstead Heath Station, the open acres have, quite frankly, been stripped of most of their original charm (nothing else is being talked about in the village inns). Horse lovers that they undoubtedly are, the locals (unlike the Fred Russells of this world) are thanking God for having created the motor car at such a convenient moment in history, for the real, socially-pristine country where they can ride uninhibitedly to their hearts' content is now only an hour's drive away.

"'E says 'e'd like ter...marry you."

Little Frankie, as has often been commented on, was not so little. At the age of twenty months he already exhibited the scaled-down corpulence that characterised most of the male members of the Kitchener clan. His was not the sinewy, compact frame of his father. However, 'big Frankie' did not befit one so tender in years, and so the appellation 'little' continued in use until it had been well and truly outgrown.

There is much debate regarding the corruption of 'Elisabeth' into 'Aunt Libby', or plain 'Libby'. Until her dying day, Louisa maintained that it was Lottie who, unable to get her tongue around such a long name, first came out with 'Libby'. Yet the victim of this corruption always claimed that she had been re-christened by Frankie (one is inclined to believe her, given that he was a good year and a half older than his cousin). Unfortunately, Elisabeth makes no reference to this in the copious pages of her diaries. In fact, post-Louisa, pre-Heath-revelation entries are almost entirely taken up with her thoughts on Jack, whom she had rather obsessively begun to view in the light of her sister-in-law's blueish asides: it was *he* who needed a partner. Yes, her own feelings did not matter a jot. In this respect, therefore, it was imperative that she withdraw into the shadowy wings. Completely unaware that she would soon be thrust into the limelight, she once wrote,

"Virtue *is* its own reward. I must never lose sight of this wonderful dictum. What joy it gives me to see Frankie walking so sweetly, and to hear him uttering such gay sounds. This is truly love that I feel. 'Love is not love / Which alters when it alteration finds, / Or bends with the remover to remove: / O, no! it is an ever-fixed mark'. Yes yes yes! Our Shakespeare's words bear their usual hallmark of Truth. Love cannot be compared to a mathematician's cunning calculations. I have learnt to see and feel that love is simply love – no more, no less. Who dares stand up and say 'My love for my wife is more real and more potent than your love for your son'? Is dawn's light brighter than sunset's? Or does not all light reach us from the same, magnificent source?

"My heart bleeds for Jack. He has known both forms of love, and one has surely blinded him to the other. His love for Frankie has no bounds, but I know that deep within him *another* manifestation of that same love is craved for. When Rose died, I am afraid she took with her more than a child alone can replace. It is my sincerest wish that it shall not be unduly long before he meets somebody else. I only pray that there will be room in their hearts for my own, 'ever-fixed' love."

Louisa is pointing to her midriff, and smiling mischievously.

"No!" cries Elisabeth as she smiles with congratulatory disbelief. Louisa is nodding cheekily. "When?"

It is tea-time. Lottie is asleep, and Frankie is trying his best to rip a collapsable bed off the wall.

"There are *some* things, my dear, that can't be said!"

"I meant..."

"I *know* wha'cher meant, silly! It's due Christmas."

"How lovely! Does Eddie know yet?"

Louisa shakes her head. "Lady does. Told 'er this mornin'."

"Oh, I'm so happy for you! And Jack will be too."

It was later that afternoon, while Elisabeth was busy preparing supper, that Frankie registered his hitherto unsuspected dislike or fear of the imposing wardrobe in the bedroom. As his aunt was later to recount to Jack, little Frankie was playing happily with his favourite wooden doll "when he started shrieking. I rushed in and found him inside. How he opened it I'll never know. Poor thing was inconsolable...shaking like a leaf." After much biting of lower lip; frowning of brow, and pacing of floor, Jack made a momentous decision. "Dad can 'ave the timber, an' those tha's needy can 'ave wha's inside." The mausoleum and its contents were summarily disposed of. It was eventually replaced by Edward and Louisa's old wardrobe, which, in order to meet the inevitable demands their new arrival would make, was in turn replaced by a much larger piece of furniture.

In such mundane ways is the influence of the very young and the unborn felt.

Mr Ernest V. Laurence, who, for reasons best known to himself, had reached the pinnacle of middle-age as a devout bachelor, was not in the long and distinguished tradition of melodramatic leading men. Broadness of shoulders, compactness of waist, and steely squareness of jaw were physical attributes he conspicuously lacked. Moreover, his eyes were not blue, or forged with virile sensitivity. The few hairs that he possessed served only to emphasize the bare rotundity of his pate. And although he was by no means short, twenty odd years of fawning service to the community had left him with a pronounced hunch.

Following his unprecedented, not to say unexpected proposal of marriage, this unsightly protuberance entered a new dimension of parabolic obsequiousness. Chance meetings with his fair damsel (in the street or in the shop) were marked by a ritual display of ingratiating dorsal arches.

Unbeknown to all concerned, he had been besotted with Elisabeth since he first set eyes on her at Jack and Rose's wedding, and had been on the verge of declaring his infatuation when Rose died. Discretion being the better part of valour, he deemed it only right and proper that he should bide his time.

In the wake of the Revelation on the Heath, Elisabeth lost her appetite, and fell prey to insomnia. What little sleep was had during that period contained frightful images of cloying hands and servile stoops. In her restless delirium, she became convinced that she was like a character in a Greek tragedy, forced by the Fates to suffer the inevitable consequences of her innate flaws. She grew resentful of Louisa, the tantalising serpent that had slithered into her modest paradise. She blamed herself for having toyed with the idea of sampling the fruits intimated to her. But when she caught herself resenting Rose for having died; when she heard her father's voice asking "Woncha regre' it?", she clenched her fists, and, peering into a looking-glass, told herself: "Elisabeth Kitchener, pull yourself together! Remember the words, those beautiful words, and never flinch from the truth again... 'Love is not love / Which alters when it alteration finds.' Act like Cordelia, not Ophelia. Behave as a woman should... Rose, please forgive me!"

When Jack returned from work that evening, his sister handed him a sealed envelope. "Please take this to Mr Laurence at once."

Not for the first time in his life, Jack felt somewhat confused. Since losing Rose, his morale had understandably plummeted, and it had been with Elisabeth's unbending support that he had resolved to raise it up each day like a sail hoisted against the wind. Rose was constantly in his thoughts. The first few weeks had been filled with visions of a cold, staring face congealed in death. Gradually, though, the face began thawing back to life, and the complicated process of letting her go (in a manner and at a pace that were tolerable) could finally commence. As bad luck would have it, this process was nowhere near completion when Mr Laurence asked for Elisabeth's hand. Jack was as shocked as his sister. His employer was a good, decent man – of that there was no doubt. In fact, the respect in which he had always been held by Jack and Rose can be gleaned from their decision to use 'Laurence' as their son's middle name. And yes, he was a man of not inconsiderable means – that too was an important consideration. Of course it was, but equally important was the consideration of age. Mr Laurence was old enough to be Elisabeth's father. Problems, problems... From one day to the next, his unbending supporter had gone off her food. Within a week, painfully reminiscent rings had appeared under her eyes, and even more painfully reminiscent, her cheeks had lost all their colour. Now: the envelope. And not a word of explanation, just "take it to him at once".

Since divulging his burning secret, Mr Laurence had taken Jack into his confidence as never before. Whenever there were no customers in the shop, he would turn to his employee with anxious, beseeching eyes, and whisper, "Are you sure she still hasn't made up her mind?" The official go-between invariably responded with a sympathetic shake of the head. This procedure began every morning with pent-up anxiety on the one side, and reluctant negation on the other. As the day wore on, it slowly unwound in intensity like a coiled spring. But all that was over. While he made his way back down the bitterly-cold, gaslit high road clutching his sister's letter, he wondered if he was the bearer of glad or sad tidings (from all their respective points of view, for despite respecting and liking the man, it was Jack's hope that Elisabeth had politely declined his marital offer. He realised that he was still emotionally dependent on her, and that this dependence would remain a heavy one until the little matter of coming to terms with Rose's death had been sorted out for good).

A measure of Jack's state of confusion at the time is the peculiar fact that he had not stopped to consider the legal implications of a such a marriage, namely, that Mr Laurence would become Frankie's legal guardian. The same, of course, could not be said of Elisabeth.

Dear Mr Laurence,

I sincerely hope that you will forgive my long silence. I must confess that I was very taken aback by the proposal you entrusted with Jack. My mind, you shall be pleased to know, is now made up. As a man of your experience will appreciate, any decision affecting my own life affects Frankie and his father. Everything and anything that I therefore decide to do must be tempered by this knowledge. Providence has taken Frankie's natural mother from us. Who, Mr Laurence, am I, or your good self, to take away his natural father? My love for Frankie is also my love for his best interests. The proposition I have to make to you is this (please do not think me ruthless or perverse): I shall agree to become your wife on the condition that Frankie, while not becoming your son, shall inherit as your son; that you shall have no say in his upbringing; that you shall recognise Jack's indefeasible claim to his son, and that you shall never wilfully obstruct its expression. If you find these conditions impossible to comply with, then I am afraid that there is no more to be said on the matter. If, on the other hand, the opposite is the case, they must be sworn to before a commissioner of oaths. Finally, I shall expect you to consider my acceptance of marriage null and void if Jack fails to give it his blessing.

Elisabeth Kitchener

A rectangular sheet of paper divided into four sections by sharply-defined creases floats gently to the floor. A jubilant superior urges his adjutant to read it.

"Well, Jack my boy, what do you say?"

From adjutant to adjudicator in one fell swoop. The sudden transition renders him speechless.

"Well?"

Yes, this has to be a dream. Any moment now he will wake up. "Overcome, eh?"

Why don't the counter and the shelves and the jars of sweets upon the shelves and Mr Laurence melt slowly into the familiar surroundings of his bedroom? Rose would be there beside him...

"Jack! Have you been struck dumb!"

"Sorry, I..."

"Well, are you or aren't you in agreement?"

"I..." Never before have his words been waited on with such an air of expectancy. "I...think I'd like ter...speak to 'er firs'."

"Oh... Very well. I've hung on this long, I can wait another night. Go home and sleep on it. Let me have your answer in the morning."

"Yes, Mr Laurence."

A pock-marked road shimmering with trapped water; a tremulous constellation of gaslights in the inverted firmament of the night; a cold, gnawing wind. The person he is most dependent on for survival is dependent on *him* for a decision. How can a dependant be expected to assume responsibility all of a sudden? Why has it all been left up to him? But if she has Frankie's future in mind, what will she think of him if he puts his foot down (orange glows are splintered) and says no. What would Mr Laurence, kind man that he is, think of him? If he's not good enough for his sister, he's not good enough to work for. And what then?

The dancing, stellular reflections underfoot have led him to a once-familiar port of call.

"Pin' of yer bes', please luv."

"Blimey, ain' seen you 'ere in donkeys...Jack, ain' it?"

The senescent face behind the paint is smiling. A senescent arm slides a glass across a polished top. Its contents are downed. A finger points to the pump.

"Never rains," remarks she of the coated, wizened countenance.

An oversized beauty-spot on one half of her cleavage catches his attention. "Wha' can I ge' yer?" he asks, shifting his gaze to her pale blue eyes.

"Tha's very decen' of yer. I'll 'ave a drop of rum if tha's alrigh' with you."

He nods. In the mirror opposite: ruddy, bloated faces bonneted by the loops and frills of stylised household names; the sebaceous back of the smiling, painted face; a neglected piano with yellow, nicotined teeth; dejection, confusion, profound, incurable grief.

"Wha's up with you, then?" The lips are stained with rum.

"I ain' go' a care in the world."

Viewed through the inside of the glass, the beauty-spot seems twice as large. He milks the last drop then hands her the glass.

"Same again?"

He nods.

"Like I said, it never rains."

Someone stumbles, falling awkwardly. The event is captured on the mirror, which also records the synchronised turning of heads. With the exaggerated care of the inebriated, a man picks himself up. Mumbling his apologies, he tries brushing off the sawdust that clings to his wet clothes. Jack takes the man by the arm and leads him to a small table in the corner, by the piano.

"Don' waste yer time on 'im, 'e's a los' cause." The advice proffered from behind the bar is greeted with throaty chuckles of approval.

"Yer in a righ' state!" Jack berates the man, turning his back on all the on-lookers.

"Jacko, ol' son! You're..." The belch reeks of pot-still whisky. "You're the las' person in the world... Wha' y'avin'? Le' me..." Clumsy hands sunk into empty pockets. "I won' be a..."

"Fred, I think y'ave 'ad enough for one nigh'."

"Couldda sworn I 'ad some... Never mind. Moll knows me. I gotta slate as long as an 'orse's dooda... Moll!"

"Yes, me pride and joy?"

"Wait 'ere," Jack instructs him, making his way across the sawdust. "Give us a pin', luv. Anna 'alf for Fred."

"Don' tell me 'e's a mate of yours." Black-rimmed eyes looking askance at the dishevelled lump in the corner. "'Arf's as good to 'im as a thimbleful." Pulling the pump.

"Well, it's all 'e's 'avin'. Wha'abou' you? Anuvver rum?"

"Thanks very much." Coaxing out the final drop in her glass with the resplendent tip of her tongue. "It's not often we ge' a gen'leman in 'ere." Stroking the pump.

A series of discordant notes triggers off a chorus of laughter. Jack hurries back to his impatient companion. The sebaceous back flexes with blithe resignation.

"Tol' yer I 'ad credit 'ere, din' I?" says Fred, proudly picking up the pint glass.

"Oh no you don'!" Jack passes him the diminutive measure. "*Tha's* your one."

"Moll put yer up to this, didn' she? You wai' till I..."

"Si'down, Fred!"

A powerful clench keeps him anchored to his seat. Emulating the mirrored torso, he resigns himself to his abstemious plight.

"Beggars can' be choosers I s'ppose." He raises his glass in a half-hearted toast.

"Cheers," responds Jack, bringing the glass to his lips. As he surveys the saloon through his glass, the focal point of his attention is, once again, a beauty-spot pulsating with feline regularity.

"'Ard times these, Jacko!" remarks Fred with a rueful look at his empty glass. "'Ere, you'll never guess," he adds, hiccupping gleefully, "wha' 'appened to 'ol Jim, you know, downa Lion." Jack shakes his head absent-mindedly. He has never heard of the man. "Go' run over by a bus! Fla' as a bleeding pancake. Ain' tha' 'ow Rose's ol' man..." The expression on Jack's face sends a shudder down his spine. "I'm sorry, Jacko, I didn' mean ter... It's jus' I ain' meself these days. Since ol' Toby's legs packed up I ain' done a stroke o'work – th'ain' like me, is it? An' t'cap it all," belching and hiccupping in quick succession, "bloody geezers downa labour exchange expec' yer t'show up every bleedin' day t'sign on. 'Ow the 'ell they expec' yer t'fine any work when yer down there all day I dunno." Jack's expression has softened, but he remains silent. "Bes' 'orse I ever 'ad, Toby. Never gave me any trouble. Luvly 'orse 'e was. Then 'e star'ed goin' lame on me. Firs' one leg, thenee uvver. I cried me eyes ou' the day I 'ad t'take 'im downa knacker's yard. 'E 'ad this look on 'is face. I swear 'e knew, hones' t'God, Jacko..."

Taking advantage of this sobering reminiscence, Jack helps his friend onto his feet. After wrapping an arm across his shoulders, he escorts him out of the Cock Tavern, across the wind-swept high road, and into Eresby Mews. By the time his clothes have been removed, the former carman has sunk into a deep slumber. Even in the dark, the squalor in which he lives is depressingly evident to Jack. The cold, damp quarters are impregnated with the stench of old manure seeping through from the abandoned stable below. Filled with a mixture of pity and anger, Jack removes his overcoat and lays it over the snoring Fred.

As unperturbed by the inclement conditions as he was earlier in the evening, Jack, his face set hard with determination, makes his unhurried way back to number 221. The lights in the shop have been extinguished. There are no signs of life in the upstairs rooms either. Jack searches in vain for some pebbles. Spurred by a decisiveness that has long been alien to him, he lobs a half-penny piece at the windows overhead. This age-old custom is repeated several times until, at last, amid a flutter of curtains, a window is opened.

"What's going on down there!"

"It's me!"

"Jack...What the blazes are you..."

"The answer's yes, all righ'?"

The hand that has been defying the efforts of the wind to dispossess him of his nightcap is relieved of duty by a flabbergasted Mr Laurence. Looking unnervingly like a cotton jellyfish, the nightcap sails off into the darkness.

"Jack, I'm so..."

But he too has been swallowed up by the night.

"Two rums."

"Where's yer friend?" inquires Moll, the scent of fermented sugar-cane still on her breath.

"Sleepin' like a baby." He looks around the saloon. There are only a few, diehard drinkers left. "Where *is* everyone?"

"I expec' they're sleepin' like babies too."

"When d'yer close up?"

"In abou' ten minutes, give or take a rum or two."

"Nigh', Moll!" cries a middle-aged man whom the corner of the bar has faithfully propped up for the past four hours.

"Nigh', Alf!" She turns towards the mirror and reaches for a three-quarter-full bottle situated above it. "I know where we can finish this in our own good time." She leans forward onto crossed arms. Apparently fated to be magnified, the beauty-spot is directly behind the thick glass of the bottle.

"Oh yeah? An' wha' abou' yer ol' man?"

"Been dead for donkeys," she says, pouring them both another drink. "Copped it inna Boer War."

"You always on yer own, then?"

"Lan'lord's a lazy so-an'-so. Only shows up Sa'adees an' Sundees. Tell yer the truth, I'm bet'er off withou' 'im."

"Wha' abou' drunks an' tha'?"

"I can 'andle 'em no trouble. Believe it or not, they're scared of ol' Moll... Wha' abou' you?"

"I ain' scared of yer."

"No, wha' I meant was will yer missus be..."

"No, she won'." He downs the rum and serves himself another. "Wha' time is it?"

"Time I was closin' up."

With a lithe vitality that is more in keeping with her youthful veneer, Moll ushers out the few remaining regulars, wipes down the tables, rearranges the chairs, and rinses the last batch of glasses. After putting out the lights, she whispers, very-matter-of-factly, "This way, Jack." A swing door leads into an unlit stairway. "Give us yer 'and. They're steep." Instead, Jack places the neck of the rum bottle in her palm. Ripples of laughter merge with the sound of creaking wood. At the top of the stairs, Moll raises a finger to her lips. "Ssshh!" She opens a door, and the sound of laboured breathing betrays the presence of at least one sleeper. Jack is guided carefully through a maze of furniture. Another door is opened. "Le'me fine the lamp." She lights it. "There we are!" The room is barely large enough to accommodate one single bed and a battered chest of drawers. Empty bottles litter the floor. "Si'down," she tells him, patting the mattress which already bears her own weight. Taking the bottle of rum from him, she puts it to her mouth. Some of the rum trickles down the side of her chin, smearing her make-up. She wipes it away with the back of her hand, smearing the grease-paint even more. The bottle is returned to Jack, sitting uneasily on the edge of the bed. "Pu' yer fee' up."

"Who's in there?" he asks, pointing to the adjoining room.

"Me mum... She's get'in' on now, an' Vicky, tha's me girl, so we bet'er not make too much noise."

"Why didn' yer tell me you..."

"Don' let 'em bovver yer," interrupts Moll, taking his hand and pulling him towards her. "They know bet'er than t'come in 'ere this time o'nigh'." She runs her fingers through his hair before pressing him to her bosom. "Don' yer worry 'bout a thin'," she reassures him, kissing the crown of his head. "Moll'll take care of yer." When he surfaces, he notices that the beauty-spot has disappeared. Giggling like a young child, Moll peels it off his forehead. "Y'ave been after it all nigh', aincha? you naugh'y thin'..." Poker-faced, Jack takes a swig from the almost empty bottle. "All righ', Mr 'Ard-ter-get, feas' yer mince pies on these!" Two large, doughy breasts are bared with obvious pride, and the beauty-spot repositioned on the granular cusp of one of them. Alas, it is not the floppy sacs that catch her visitor's eye, but the folded handkerchief that had been wedged discreetly between the two. His fascination with the dislodged square of pink material does not pass unnoticed. By way of an explanation, Moll cups her breasts, and, drawing each to one side, informs him that the handkerchief serves to prevent chafing. "Big girls' secre'," she adds with a smile that is intended to be voluptuous.

"Where d'yer ge' it?"

"Why all this fuss over an 'ankie?" He picks it up. "If yer mus' know, I go' it downa marke'place." Fearing the worst, he unfolds it. "Wha's come over yer! Y'ave gone as pale as a..." He heads for the door. "Where d'yer fink yer goin'?" The door closes behind him.

The obstacles in his path are negotiated with the disconcerting accuracy of a sleepwalker. The sound of doors being unbolted confirms the definitive nature of his hasty and inexplicable retreat. Disconsolate, irate, Moll gulps down the last of the rum. Breaking wind with a satisfying vengeance, she stares at the handkerchief beside her. What on earth could he have... Unable or, perhaps, unwilling to resist a sudden urge, she grabs it and buries her nose in its soft folds. The acrid perfume inhaled with deep, deep breaths is gratifyingly arousing. Slowly, very slowly, a senescent arm guides a hand towards a melting peak capped with a beauty-spot. "Beggars can' be choosers," she thinks, echoing the sentiments of one of her finest customers as the pink square is transferred to lower, marshland regions. Running her tongue over rum-moist lips; inhaling her own, secreted smells; shallower and shallower of breath, an embroidered 'R' is applied with frenzied precision to the turgid area that beckons.

Three

Lady, Frank and the rest of the fast-expanding Kitchener family were shocked by the news of Elisabeth's betrothal. The topics of Louisa's pregnancy, the progress of Charlotte and Frankie, and Jack's state of mind were supplanted overnight by her decision to wed the ageing confectioner. Concerted efforts were made to dissuade her, and she at once became a walking target for a barrage of "Woncha regre' its" and "Think of the futures". "'E's old enough to be yer favver" was also fired at her if the first two failed to make any impact (as they invariably did). Elisabeth, to continue in bellicose vein, stuck to her guns, and, as so often happens in these situations, the more they tried to change her mind, the more determined she became. Typically, Louisa adopted a different kind of offensive altogether. During one of their regular walks together, she took careful aim and said, "They reckon it, you know, don' work so well after a certain age." "Yes," retorted Elisabeth, who by now could dodge an on-coming bullet with the greatest of ease, "it is a source of great concern to me that Mr...that Ernest is not at least ten years older than he is."

While real bullets were riddling real Bulgarians with real holes, the Kitcheners launched a fierce, do-or-die attack on the one person who, they were convinced, could bring Elisabeth to her senses. Yet, parental, brotherly and sisterly pressure was once again applied in vain. Not only was Jack unwilling to scupper the marriage plans, but he was actually in favour of them (*How could you! She's almost half his age*), and he had even agreed to act as best man (*What will people say?*).

How could he explain his reasons when he himself did not

understand them? Since the unforgettable night of swirling medusas and enlarged moles, Jack had begun to regard his sister with growing admiration. Her unselfish motives; her strength of character, and her devotion to Frankie were no longer taken for granted. Above all, he sensed that she was doing the right thing – that Rose would have approved.

As stipulated, the nuptial vows were preceded by the taking of 'Elisabethan' vows by the bridegroom. Before a slightly-bewildered commissioner, Mr Laurence made the oaths required of him. Binding quill was put to paper, and a date for the marriage was set: the last Saturday of May, 1913. In the intervening months, Elisabeth paid frequent visits to the flat above the sweet-shop. Its large rooms seemed dull and rather oppressive to her. It would take a lot of work to wipe away the layers of unimaginative bachelorhood. Mr Laurence did not take umbrage at this. Quite the contrary, he revelled in it. Every fresh display of what he described as the 'feminine touch' was greeted with appreciative awe. "I just don't know how I managed to put up with it for so long the way it was!" This became his stock phrase during those days.

Anxious to study Mr Laurence at closer quarters, Louisa would often accompany Elisabeth on her excursions to her future home. On such occasions, Lottie's pram doubled as a miniature removals van, transporting an array of bits and pieces. On her first visit, she had made straight for the bedroom, where a brand new double-bed had already been installed. Bouncing up and down on the mattress, she gave Elisabeth her nodded approval. But she was not so approving of the Ecce Homo that hung above it on the wall. "Don' think *I* could sleep at nigh's with tha' thin' over me 'ead." Elisabeth's passion for drama had enured her to such scenes of suffering, and she would not be persuaded to take it down. Late one afternoon, however, Louisa came across something that did ruffle her sister-in-law. "Take a look at this!" she whispered, full of intrigue. She had been rummaging through an old trunk in the hall, and had found a photograph of an extremely beautiful woman. "Read wha' it says." Elisabeth's entry for that day picks up the story,

"'To my dear Ernest, with my neverending love.' Why was my heart filled with the hemlock of jealousy on reading those words? If I had been steered by the hand of love towards him I would have well understood my reaction. Or are Cupid's tricks so well disguised? Louisa is convinced that it is a mistress, at best a long-forgotten one; at worst... One reads about such women. I was too embarrassed to ask him about it today, but if I fail to confront him with it I shall never have peace of mind."

The following morning, on the pretext that she needed his advice on an important matter, she asked Mr Laurence to join her upstairs.

"Now then," he said with a businesslike sigh, "what's the problem?"

Composing herself, she replied, "Oh, it's not really a problem...it's about a photograph."

"A photograph? Elisabeth, can't this wait? Jack's down there on his own and..."

"I know I'm being silly, but...well, I just can't decide where to hang a photograph I found yesterday in the trunk." She examined his face for tell-tale signs. "Know the one I mean?"

"No, I can't say I do. Where is it?"

"Here," she answered, producing it from behind her back.

Mr Laurence looked at it with suspicious fondness. "Good Lord! I haven't set eyes on that picture for years. Yes! Let's hang it up somewhere. What a good idea, Elisabeth."

"You could at least tell me who it's of."

"It's my mother! Who did you think it was, my mistress?"

"Don't be silly."

The betrothed maiden smiled awkwardly.

Other preparations were afoot. Since the unforgettable night of the sawdust and nicotined pianos, not a day went by without Fred Russell receiving a visit from his bereaved friend. At first, the visits were formal and rather strained, the sort paid by dutiful neighbours. But gradually, as each man grew more adept at making the other feel comfortable, they developed into relaxed, lighthearted affairs. More often than not, they would go on to Eresby Road, where Elisabeth had started setting an extra place for supper. So touched was Fred by the unaffected care showered on him that he felt honour-bound not to let the Kitcheners down in any conceivable way. With this firmly in mind, he stayed well clear of public houses. He even began paying back what he owed at his old haunts. And on the odd occasion when temptation did manage to get the better of him, it pricked his conscience to such an extent as to completely mar the experience, rendering it less and less palatable each time.

Much to his pleasant surprise, but seeming the obvious compromise to everyone in the family, it was eventually suggested to Fred that he move in with Jack when Elisabeth and Frankie vacated the property.

"Dunno wha'a say, Jacko!"

"Jus' say yes before I change me mind."

"I do."

A white veil is raised like a visor. A ritualistic kiss is carefully executed. A clan looks on with very mixed emotions. An organ sounds a welcome retreat.

That very night, a man returned to the bed on which a mother had lost what she had given, and a collapsable structure on sturdy hinges moaned under a new weight.

Elsewhere, matrimonial life was initiated beneath a crown of thorns.

In one of those strange ironies of life, Jack saw a great deal more of his son than when the two of them lived under the same roof. The truth of the matter was that they had only really been able to see each other at length on Sundays. The rest of the week was not conducive to anything more than the odd exchange of smiles and coos, given that Jack was at work for most of the day. Since the move, however, father and toddler spent whole hours together at the shop. While the one served behind the counter, or toiled in the stock-room at the rear of the premises, the other would happily play by his side. The 'little' one soon became a firm favourite with the majority of customers, who warmed to his golden locks and his soft, cherubic sturdiness. But, regrettably, there was a tiny minority that looked on the unusual arrangement, of which the child was a constant reminder, as morally unsound. Unable to come to terms with this, these customers did the decent thing and refrained from purchasing Mr Laurence's wares. The effect on the weekly takings was minimal.

Fred was still unemployed. Although Edward had managed to persuade his foreman to find room for an extra labourer, he was dismissed after just one day. An old drinking colleague working on the site taunted him about his reformist ways, and never one to suffer ridicule (at least when sober), Fred responded with an articulate blow to the head. Both his taunter and his career as a builder were out for the count. The problem with Fred was that he loved horses. The problem with horses was that they invariably loved *him*. Needless to say, he would have made the perfect equerry. There was only one possible solution. Shortly after Frankie's second birthday, and unbeknown to Fred, Jack paid a visit to Richard Annenberg. The sporting outfitter had recently opened a new shop on the sophisticated slopes of the Heath, and was therefore ideally placed to help. Mr Laurence, who was most impressed by Jack's concern for his friend, posed no objections when his new brother-in-law asked him if he could take the afternoon off. "Good cause, Jack – good cause," he said, patting him on the back. "Oh, and don't forget to give my regards to Dickie." As Jack boarded the Hampstead train, accompanied by Frankie, who had insisted on going, he was suddenly struck by the thought that the thing which determined whether life's challenges were problematic or exciting was simply one's attitude to them. This was not a thought in the strict sense of the word, but rather a heartfelt conviction. Moreover, he sensed that, ultimately, the more effort he invested in living, the easier and less painful it would be to accept Rose's death.

Hampstead Heath Station was thronging with holiday-makers. It was Friday, a midsummer afternoon, and many people had clearly taken the day off work in the hope of missing the even bigger crowds that the weekend was sure to wash up on the sought-after slopes. Holding Frankie's hand very tightly, Jack waded his way to Fitzjohn's Avenue, where the crowds began to disperse. Brilliant sunshine filtered through the thick foliage in greens and yellows. The tree-lined avenue, with its impressive houses, seemed a lot further from Kilburn than a ten-minute train ride.

Despite his more positive frame of mind, Jack could do nothing to allay the butterflies fluttering in his stomach as he entered the shop and a piercing bell announced his arrival. A young lady balanced demurely on a stool was busy arranging boxes on the highest of the many shelves behind the counter. She looked him up and down before indicating that she would attend to him as soon as possible. The smell of leather hung in the air like pipe tobacco. Everything around them was so polished that it was difficult to imagine how anyone could have the heart to actually lay a finger on them: golf clubs, riding crops, saddles... When the young lady had completed her undeferable task she climbed down and disappeared into a back-room without uttering a word. She re-emerged after a few minutes, her hands clasped in front of her.

"How can I help you?"

"I'd, um, like a word with Mr Annenberg, please."

"I'm afraid that Mr Annenberg is busy at the moment."

Jack frowned and gazed nervously at his feet. He had not anticipated this. "I 'ave ter...It's impor'an' I see 'im. I'm a frien' of Mr Laurence's – in Kilburn."

"Wait here, please," said the young lady, sighing her disapproval.

Her demeanour did nothing to appease the butterflies, but quite impervious to his father's anxieties, Frankie helped himself to one of the many riding crops sprouting from a copper container.

"Pu' tha' back!" ordered Jack, fearing the implement would be irreparably soiled.

"It's all right, let him play with it." Mr Annenberg was smiling. "Good to see you again... It's Jack, isn't it?"

"Yes."

"So, how's the old rascal, then? I hear he's finally tied the knot."

"Yes. 'E sends 'is..."

"And who's this little fellow?"

"My lit'le boy."

"He looks like you. Miss Nichols, see if you can keep him amused while I talk to Jack, will you? Now then, what can I do for you?"

"It's abou' a frien' of mine who's – 'e used t'be...the thin' is, 'e gets on with 'orses like an 'ouse on fire. Knows 'em inside ou'. Since 'is las' one wen' lame 'e's been like a fish ou' of wa'er. If

only 'e could ge' another job workin' with 'em... So I though'
tha', well, seein' as yer mus' know lots of people...if it wasn' too
inconvenien', yer migh' be able t'ask aroun' an'..."

"Yes, I see," said a ponderous Mr Annenberg, pursing his lips.
"You say he has a way with horses."

"Always 'as 'ad – it's a gift 'e's go'."

"Leave it with me, Jack. I'll see what I can do and let you know,
all right?"

"Tha's really kine of you, Mr..."

"Nonsense, it's no trouble at all... And I see we have a jockey
in the making!" observed Mr Annenberg with a wry smile after a
riding crop had been slashed with infantile relish across the rump
of a horrified young mare.

With twelve months still to go before the cameras and the
tanks start rolling, the bellicose swelling is beginning to show.
Yet the honest folk of Kilburn and Willesden are largely
unconcerned about this. What the microcosmic eye does not see
(or cannot or will not or is prevented from seeing), the microcosmic heart does not feel. But the honest folk of Kilburn and
Willesden *are* concerned about something, for it has been
thoughtfully brought to their attention by lay and clerical
authorities alike that suspicious-looking men in motor cars are
making concerted efforts to recruit local parish girls into the
White Slave Trade. These abominable attempts have so outraged
the community that even the proposed building of a smallpox
hospital in nearby Kingsbury has paled into insignificance. There
is no shortage of sermons on the Shoot-up-hill or Kensal Rise by
incensed parsons. Members of Parliament are not far behind in
this respect, as speech after speech is delivered in packed church
halls. No parents worth their salt allow their daughters to walk
the streets unaccompanied. No citizen worthy of the name turns
a blind eye whenever a motor car bearing suspicious-looking
males cruises by at an unusually slow speed. And of course, no
constable with an ounce of integrity stands idly by while girls
engage in conversation with men in parked vehicles.

Who can estimate the adverse effects on parents' health
occasioned by the late arrival of one of their daughters? What
manner of sexually explicit visions have descended on thus-

plagued fathers and mothers as a result of this much-feared recruitment campaign? One can but hazard a guess. We do know, however, that the rumours of its existence are not unfounded. Mary Kitchener, a blooming English rose aged nineteen, is one of the few who has lived to tell the tale. The lascivious attentions of two vehicled members of the opposite sex were directed towards her in the broadest of daylight as she was making her way home after visiting her sister Elisabeth. Mary, who had chosen to model herself on her only sister-in-law (a decision more subliminal than conscious), had acquired a reputation for "being keen on boys". Consequently, each time the Kitcheners were assembled in numbers, such as at Christmas, birthdays or weddings (but excepting funerals), her "keenness" became the butt of extremely bland jokes and asides. Not surprisingly, the perpetrators of these slurs on her character were not exactly quick to react sympathetically when Mary related her experience to them. Her younger brothers and sisters were united in their refusal to believe a single word she said, and teased her about it for days. Frank and his son Edward cast knowing looks when she pleaded her innocent involvement in the matter. Not so Jack, Elisabeth, Louisa, and the stooping brother-in-law: they gave welcome credence to her version of events.

"I'd jus' turned inter Victoria Road, mindin' me own business, when this really ol' Napier screeches to an 'alt nex'a me. I go' a real shock, bu', still, I though' nothin' of it when the driver asked me the way t'Maida Vale. 'E 'ad dark 'air an' eyes, an' one of them dimples some men've go' in their chins, an' 'e migh've been foreign. Any'ow, 'is friend was. Couldda been Arab or somethin'. Yer goin' the wrong way, I says, an' then 'is friend said somethin' 'bout earnin' lots of money in the sun. Tha's when I realised they were white slave traders. I mustta gone all pale or somethin' cos one of 'em asked me if I was all righ'. Become a princess, they said, get'in' ou' the car. Tha's it, I though', I've 'ad it. Me legs seized up an' I knew I'd never see any of you again. Then, thank God, this bobbie comes roun' the corner an' they jumped in their car an' roared off. So I tells the bobbie, righ', an' guess wha': 'e laughs 'is 'ead off. Says 'e can' do 'is beat

no more withou' someone like me comin' up to 'im cryin' blue
murder."

Of such negligent individuals are otherwise perfectly sound
constabularies made.

There can be no doubt that some stones, like graves, are best
left unturned. The sacrificial associations of the Ecce Homo in
the Laurence bedroom were therefore intended to say it all, but,
on reflection, it is obvious that symbolic hints can only go so far
in the conveyance of certain, delicate truths. Subtle clues and
pointers in these intimate matters will not satisfy the devout
reader of fiction, whose thirst for knowledge in the field of
human behaviour and psychology demands detail, not inference;
descriptive valour, not discretion. So it is for them, and them
alone, that we roll the boulder of discreet insinuation onto its
side and contemplate what lies exposed with the morbid fascination of a child who, turning over an old brick in the garden,
is confronted with a wriggling mass of insects...

Can the suffering of a young woman on her wedding night
be justifiably compared to the suffering of a young man nailed
to a cross? If one were able to somehow extract their respective
agonies with a syringe, and deposit them on a scale, which would
weigh more? The old question 'Which is heavier, a pound of
feathers or a pound of sand?' comes to mind. A pound is a
pound. Suffering is suffering. The comparison is also justifiable
on the grounds of love. Although one should not believe all that
one reads, it is commonly held that the crucified man sacrificed
his life because of his love for mankind. Did not the young
woman in question sacrifice her life because of her love for a
nephew? Furthermore, if we accept that a measure of weight and
suffering are constant factors, cannot the same be said of love,
that 'ever-fixed mark'? And what of the spear which, according
to informed sources, was driven into the ailing man's side? Was
not the young woman similarly assailed in keeping with matrimonial tradition? Did she not bleed too? You will see for your-
selves, for, after all, that is the desired purpose of the exercise.

Let us proceed, then, with surreptitious tread to the sacrificial
altar. Careful, this door creaks a bit. Stay close to me. High heels

should be removed and carried, but be careful you don't drop them. Now, steady does it. Place your feet exactly where I do, otherwise we run the risk of giving ourselves away. I know these floorboards like the back of my hand. We'll hide in the corner, away from the light seeping in from the high road – there, under that photograph of Mr Laurence's mother. Good... There they are. See them? She's already in bed, and he's undressing with an air of strained joviality. *What* cradle? No, of course not. Frankie's no longer a baby, remember? He has his own room now. Notice how she's looking the other way. Yes, that *is* a girdle he's wearing. Vanity is ageless, I suppose. He's coming towards us. Keep still!

Neatly-folded clothes are stored away in a large wardrobe redolent of mothballs. Mr Laurence shuts the door and turns the small key in the lock to stop it swinging open. He crosses the room to where his virgin bride awaits upon a virgin bed. The moment could not be more solemn, and as the covers are drawn reverently back, his bogus joviality is drowned in a sudden exudation of cold sweat. The feverish trepidation is triggered by the knowledge that the waiting is well and truly over. There, within inches of his clammy grasp, are the veiled contours of womanhood. He slides in, wiping his palms on the crisp linen. Elisabeth remains still. For a few seconds that feel like an eternity to Mr Laurence, he lies motionless on his side of the bed. Only the sound of his fast-accelerating breath can be heard in the street-lit room. But as the cold perspiration accentuates the adjacent warmth, and the smell of freshly-soaped skin wafts up freshly-trimmed nostrils, the crucifixion can be delayed no longer. Mumbling "Elisabeth, I..." he reaches out his hand, making contact with a wall of shrouded stomach muscles. Fearing that the momentum will be lost unless his physical declaration is rapidly backed up by another, he searches out her lips. In the process, his shoulder levers painfully against her right breast, causing her to wince. This is interpreted by Mr Laurence as a positive response to his declared intentions, whereupon his weight is brought to bear on her with extra vigour. Whispering a series of 'Elisabeths', Mr Laurence gathers up the long folds of her nightdress with passionate haste. The countdown has commenced. Elisabeth poses no resistance. Her brutal vulnerability has to be endured, and the sooner the ordeal is over, the better. Mr Laurence has redirected his resources to the task of locating the enticing entrance. After several unsuccessful attempts, he manages to find it, but he also finds, to his horror, that it is hermetically sealed. Swivelling awkwardly on his ungirdled abdomen, he tries in vain to consummate his marriage. "Elisabeth, help me!" He is desperately aware that the pulsating surge inside of him is gathering force; that he is losing the fight against time. Ten, nine... His plea has failed to achieve the 'open sesame' effect he had hoped for...eight, seven, six... But he will not be denied on this, of all nights...five, four... Larger and excruciatingly fuller than he can ever recall being, the solid appendage is fumbled into position...three... Time running out. The unyielding passage must be prised open...two... *Is* prised open...one......... Seminal ecstasy above, proportional to haemal pain below – the cruellest of equations.

Right, follow me. They won't notice us now. I'll just open the door. Mind your step. There, you've seen it with your own eyes, and heard it with your own ears. No, you can't stick your finger in the wound! Sshhh! Hear that? He actually apologised to her. Crying? No, it's not her. It's Frankie. You know what children are like in new places. She's coming to the door. It won't be the last time she'll spend the night in her nephew's bed.

No lightning and thunder. No howling gale, but that a cloistered veil was torn asunder let no one ever doubt. Now, help me push this boulder back into place...

Jack Kitchener Esq., c/o Mr Ernest V. Laurence, 221 High Road Kilburn. "Dear Jack, brief word. Turns out your friend's services are much in demand in this neck of the woods. Tell him to take this letter to Mr Charles Blishen, 18 Church Row – he's a good customer of mine. Sincerely hope it works out. Yours, Richard Annenberg."

What the butler saw: dampened strands of hair springing back unrulily from the boundaries to which a fine-toothed comb had tugged them; blue, inquisitive eyes on either side of a marginally-fractured nose; a ruddy, clean-shaven jaw whose squareness was highlighted by the striking breadth of two shoulders housed in an ill-fitting jacket; knee-worn trousers suspended from an over-tightened belt, and exposed, wrinkled socks encased in old, black boots.

"Yes?" The crumpled passport is handed over. With critical frown, the document is subjected to a rigorous examination. A well-groomed head is bowed with stylised servility. "This way please."

Antlered heads in the drawing-room stare down from the walls without the slightest trace of resentment in their glassy expressions. A marble mantelpiece buckles under the weight of gleaming, magnificently-engraved trophies, each distorting the features of the face that takes them in. Centre stage is the softest-looking sofa he has ever seen. If only he had the temerity to sit in it.

"Will Sir be wantin' anythin' to drink?"

A young maid has appeared from nowhere. Realising that she must be addressing him (there is no other person in the room), he swallows hard before replying, "Cuppa tea, please." The girl sucks in her upper lip in a reflex effort to suppress her giggles, and makes a speedy exit. Her footsteps, tap-tap-tapping in the hall, mingle with the buzz of activity emanating from various quarters of the household. On her return, she is carrying a silver tray, and is still nursing an uncontrollable urge to break into laughter.

"Does Sir take sugar?" she asks, pouring the steaming brew into a translucent cup.

"Er, yes, please. Three. Is it all righ' if I si'down?"

Both lips disappear from view. Finding it rather difficult to thus reply to his question, the risible maid has no alternative but to nod her head and arch her eyebrows affirmatively. Chinking porcelain is then placed within easy reach of the sofa. But the girl is only human. The last straw is the sheer panic which registers on the man's face as he descends into seemingly infinite depths of down...down, down... Not even the hand pressed tightly against her lips can hold back the surge of laughter as she scurries out of the room, only to collide into Mr Blishen.

"Funny girl!" he remarks as she begs his pardon on the run. "Sorry to keep you waiting. Oh please don't bother to get up," he adds as, cup in hand, Fred struggles to defy the pull of the upholstered quicksand. "So, you are Mr...?"

"Russell, Fred'rick Russell."

"Mr Russell...Well, yes..."

"Ev'ryone calls me Fred."

"Ah...Well, Fred, Dickie – that's Mr Annenberg, tells me you're a bit of a dab hand with horses."

"Worked wiv 'em all me life, Sir."

"Good...splendid...you're just the man I need. You see, even though the days when one could ride on the Heath are long gone, there's a lovely plot of land – private, of course – that belongs to a group of us. It's really for the children's sake since most of us do our riding out in the country nowadays. Start them young, I say." Is it Fred's imagination or has a group of maids *really* gathered outside the room, behind their master's back and just out of view? There are definitely streaks of movement now and then upon the gleaming surface of the trophies. "Your job, Fred, would be to look after the ponies – grooming, feeding, that sort of thing – as well as being on hand when the children were out riding. Not much to it, really – as long as you know about horses, that is. Last chappie I had couldn't tell a filly from a stud. Think you're up to it?"

"Can' wai' t'star'."

"Splendid. By the way, you'll be paid two sovereigns a week, and you'll lunch with the staff."

The trophies record a splintered explosion of movement.

Unlike her sister Mary, Elisabeth had not modelled herself (subliminally or otherwise) on the mortal likes of Louisa. Faithful, as ever, to her consecrated suitors, she had chosen to emulate the eternal likes of Cordelia (it has been observed already how the Cordelian example of forthrightness stood her in good stead when the shadow of a cringing curve plunged her into a bitter and depressive gloom). And although she was a supporter of suffragism, and never flinched from defending Mrs Pankhurst and her fellow limpets when she was in the company of deriders, she had long since resigned herself to the regrettable fact that marching up and down streets, attending rallies, and securing

herself to the railings of public buildings were not compatible
with her commitments to Frankie's upbringing. (It is yet another
of life's ironies that the latter-day daughters of the feminist
freedom fighters so staunchly defended by Elisabeth at a time
when to do so was highly unfashionable would look upon her
monomaniac motherliness as a symbol of the most insidious
problem faced by the movement: the belief that men have a God-
given right not to rear children. Nourished on an insatiable diet
of acquired rights; uncorsetted and unbrassièred, these redoub-
table post-Pankhurstians would brandish a bare, unjewelled
finger at Elisabeth and her brother, and, waxing rhetorical, pose
the following questions: is the chemical composition of the male
cuticle such that it would disintegrate on contact with an off-
spring's excrement? Is a man a latent homosexual if he dons an
apron or darns a sock? Is househusbandry an acute form of
insanity? Is masculine brawn always preferable to feminine brain
in the workplace?

There are few things more dispiriting or soul-destroying than
a sacrifice ridiculed. Fortunately, Elisabeth would not live long
enough to find herself pilloried by the changing ways of the
world.)

The said upbringing started in earnest on the 25th of June,
1913 – a day after Frankie's second birthday. Pedagogues may
argue that a child of two is, potentially, as voracious a devourer
of knowledge as a caterpillar is of foliage. However, whereas a
common grub never tires of eating leaves, it is often the case that
a bookworm in the making develops a form of mental anorexia
when subjected to an overgenerous and highly ambitious diet of
learning. Was this the reason why Frankie took to reading as
enthusiastically as a cat takes to water? Or was his complete dis-
interest in all matters aesthetic, artistic or intellectual no fault of
his early education, but rather a genetic inevitability? It is difficult to say, but, at the risk of once again deriding her sacrifice, it
has to be said that Elisabeth's decision to introduce her nephew
into the hallowed realm of Literature via Shakespeare's *King Lear*
probably did more harm than good. It goes without saying that
her judgement must have been blinded by the strong affinity she
felt for the monarch's youngest daughter, but she makes no
allusion to this in her diaries. (While on the subject of Elisabeth's

diaries, it is worth pointing out that following her marriage to Mr Laurence, her entries appear to have been penned by a different person. Not only are there notable calligraphic differences, there are stylistic ones too. Little is given away; great efforts are made to paint a picture of domestic bliss, and the entries are generally shorter. Perhaps the strangest thing of all is the fact that her entries dried up completely during the turbulent years of the war.)

Picture the peculiar scene, then: in a child's room above a high road sweet-shop, an ersatz mother reads to an infant and the three-legged horse with which he is trying to amuse himself...

"Blow, winds, and crack your cheeks! rage! blow! / You cataracts and hurricanoes, spout / Till you have drench'd our steeples, drown'd the cocks! / You sulphurous and thought-executing fires, / Vaunt-couriers to oak-cleaving thunderbolts, / Singe my white head! And thou, all-shaking thunder, / Strike flat the thick rotundity o' the world! / Crack nature's moulds, all germens spill at once/ That make ingrateful man!"

"Elisabeth...is anything the matter? I heard stamping."

Leather-bound volume in hand, she peers over her shoulder at Mr Laurence, his hand still resting timorously on the doorhandle. "There's *nothing* the matter."

"But that noise... The customers... I even heard some shouting."

"I was interpreting," she explains, pressing the book to her bosom. "Shakespeare's words were meant to be heard, not..."

"Shakespeare!" he interrupts, forgetting that he has signed away his right to a say in Frankie's education. "You're not reading him Shakespeare, are you? No wonder the poor thing looks so miserable."

A withering glare that the old king himself would have been proud of forces him to retreat from the doorway, but no sooner has Mr Laurence removed himself than Frankie lets out a woeful scream. Tears cascade down his cheeks at such a prolific rate that steeples and cocks are in danger of being drenched and drowned. Elisabeth tries to comfort him, and is reminded of the day he took a pathological dislike to the wardrobe-cum-mausoleum in Eresby Road. To her horror, though, her comforting embraces serve only to worsen his plight. For some reason that she cannot comprehend, Frankie (her little, beloved Frankie for whom she has done so...but no, virtue is its own reward...) remains inconsolable. As powerless and as vulnerable as when... She pulls away from him, and then, and only then, does she notice that his red, streaming eyes are trained on the book in her hand. On an impulse, Elisabeth buries the volume under a cushion, smiles, makes a show of her empty hands, and wraps her arms around him once again. The sobbing dies down and silence soon fills the room.

Notwithstanding this experience, however; sensitive only to the incidental fact that possibly the ranting and raving of deranged kings on pluvial heaths was not the stuff that children's stories were made of, Elisabeth would attempt to remedy the situation by switching to more lightweight works such as *Twelfth Night* – but to no avail. The little Kitchener had only to lay eyes on the dreaded leather-bound covers in Elisabeth's hands to screw up his face and start crying. It was evident that blank verse had the same effect on him that certain frequencies of light have on epileptics. With her usual sense of sacrifice, Elisabeth turned to the works of Lewis Carroll. To her dismay, Frankie's mysterious aversion persisted. In fact, there was not a single book on her shelves, or on any others, to which he did not take exception. Exercising her commendable powers of self-restraint, Elisabeth decided to postpone the literary-appreciation classes for another year. This meant that the English instructress in her would have to wait like a genie in a bottle. In the interim, however, an unsuspecting Mr William Bright, piano tuner and teacher extraordinaire, would be called upon to impart his musical expertise to an equally-unsuspecting master Frank.

The non-Pankhurstian housewives of Eresby Road had always had a soft spot for Jack Kitchener. Understandably, it had been kneaded a little softer by Rose's tragic death. There was a certain *je ne sais quoi* quality about the laconic young man who kept himself to himself. Their fascination with him, for that is what it amounted to, had intensified with the departure of Elisabeth and Frankie, and the arrival of Fred. It is no exaggeration to say that at least fifty percent of their conversations centred on Jack and his friend. Real flies on the wall were naturally unmoved by what they heard, but had there been figurative ones present, they would have been lulled very quickly into a deep slumber by a litany of adoring, if not always accurate, sentiments, "'Ow 'e's coped! Looks bet'er evry day! Nevuh grumbles, bless 'im. Mose men I know wouldda drowned their sorrows an' ended up inner doss-'ouse – bu' no' 'im, no... Marvlous wha' 'e did for 'is mate, too. I 'eard 'e got 'im a job wiv'er 'Ouse'ole Cavalry. Tha's wha' I call true frenship – the real Simon Pure tha' is. You can 'ear a pin drop when those two's in. My Bert's all admiration, 'e is. Says t'come 'ome after an 'ard day's work wiv no dinner cooked for yer, bleedin' marvlous tha' is. Course, when I can, I tries an' 'ave 'em roun' fer a bite t'eat, bu' yer can' always do tha', can yer? I mean, it's 'ard times, ain' it?"

Not bound by such restrictions, Elisabeth did her level best to help in that respect. Often, when Jack shouted his farewell up the shaft of the stairway, his sister would reply, "Just a minute, Jack! I've got something for you and Fred," whereupon an earthenware pot containing a stew or some soup would be brought down to him. Also, as was only natural, he had lunch at the shop every working day. Thus, despite the concern of their neighbours, the two men rarely went hungry. But what of their evenings? How did they amuse themselves? More often than not, they chatted and rolled tobacco (Fred did most of the chatting and most of the rolling). Neither activity came naturally to Jack, and the same was true of watching Charlton Athletic play football on occasional Saturdays, but he sensed that genuine comradeship was based on the mutual sharing of foibles (*his* foibles included reading the local paper from cover to cover before engaging in conversation every evening; going on solitary walks, and keeping his thoughts and feelings to himself).

During those final months of 1913, Fred spent many an evening regaling Jack with his adventures in the Blishen household, where, of late, there was love in the air.

"'Er name's Agaffa. Ever since the firs' day I seen 'er, I've been tryin' t'get 'er on 'er own." He draws on his cigarette, and sends a blue spiral towards Jack, seated across the table. "Any'ow, guess wha'? Today, righ', after all these monfs, I finally got 'er on 'er own. I'd jus' saddled the ponies when I sees 'er slippin' out the backer the 'ouse. There's an ol' shed nex' ter the stables. So I

creeps up an' looks in. Ya'll nevuh guess wha' she was doin',
Jacko! Smokin'! Couldn' see 'er fer smoke. Does Mr Joyce know
abou' this, I says – 'e's the butler. She jumped a mile! Nex' fing I
know she's pleadin' wiv me not ter tell 'im. You shouldda seen
'er! All over me, she was. So I says, well, I dunno. Oh please! she
says, I'll do anyfink you wan', jus' don' tell 'im. She's only sixteen,
Jacko. Tha's why I was playin' 'er up like tha'. Then I told 'er
bou' tha' firs' day, when she couldn' stop laughin' at me, an' 'ow
she'd gone an' tol' all the uvvers abou' me. She wen' brigh' red,
said she'd jus' star'ed workin' there an' was all nervous, an' tha'
she *adn'* tol' anyone bou' me. Alrigh', I says, fair dos. Wha' yer
doin' Sundee? She looked at me all funny an' laughed. There
yer go again, I told 'er. Well maybe ol' Joyce doesn' fine me so
funny. She wen' as white as a sheet an' grabbed me arm. No, I'll
do anyfink, she says, please. Alrigh', then, wha' yer doin' Sundee?
I could see 'er mine workin', tryin'a fine an excuse. So I pretends
I'm goin' back ter the 'ouse an' she nearly pulls me bleedin' arm
off! Alrigh'! she shouts. Where d'yer wan' it, 'ere? In the stables?
Nex' fing I know she's liftin' 'er ruddy skirts up. So I told 'er not
t'be so stupid. I wouldn've tol' Joyce in a monf of Sundees. All of
a sudden she's lookin' at me like I'm the Prince of Wales an' she
star's runnin' 'er 'ans through me 'air – hones' t'God, Jacko! I
ain' pullin' yer leg. It's yer lucky day, son, I tol' meself. So I makes
sure there's no one abou' an' puts me arm roun' 'er waist. Oh,
she's a luvly lit'le fing! We 'ad a grea' time in there, I can tell yer!
An' it's all fenks t'you fer get'in' me the job!"

Perhaps it never occurred to Fred. Perhaps he was too pru-
dent to voice it, but the fact of the matter is that he never asked,
"An' 'ow are *you* get'in' on in tha' depar'men', Jacko?" Since the
unforgettable night of the unfortunate pectoral wedge, Jack had
steered well clear of women: that is, his body had. There was
nothing he could possibly do to prevent the features of a beautiful girl passed in the street or served in the shop cropping up
later in his dreams. Moreover, his subconscious mind, unleashed
by sleep, and overcompensating for the celibacy for which his
famous namesake was renowned at the time, played host to a
neverending procession of scantily-dressed women. The most
recurring dream was one in which he found himself being burnt
at the stake. When the surrounding flames threatened to con-

sume him, the fire would change into a circle of dancing nymphs, their red tongues licking at his torso like viperous flames. There was only one way to quell their taunting lasciviousness: a way that he resisted and resisted until, tortured into submission, cursing their treachery, he could endure it no longer. It was always the same: violent ejaculations...fleeting dream triumph...a soiled, guilt-ridden awakening.

Those of a cynical disposition will no doubt contend that if physical Chastity gives rise to rampant eroticism in the subconscious mind, then the opposite must also be the case: physical promiscuity generating dreams and fantasies of Chastity. Such a contention may, or may not, bring a smile to our lips (that depends entirely on whether one is amused by the thought of an ardent fornicator dreaming predominantly of holy orders and solemn vows), but it does serve to highlight possibly the biggest problem facing the pure of heart and other organs: the inevitable backlash of suppressed needs or desires. This, however, is a digression, for Jack's aim was never sexual abstention and the attainment of spiritual purity. In the aftermath of his wife's death, 'keeping himself to himself' was a natural consequence, not a rational decision. Shellshocked that he was, it had taken him a considerable period of time to even think of consummating Rose's death. Much later still, when thought became a sudden, pressing urge on a night of turmoil; when it seemed as though, at last, that most important of steps towards the full acceptance of her loss would be taken, the freak revival of Rose's memory put paid to the proceedings and the prospect of more like them with such a profound sense of finality that one is tempted to speculate that if, with an almighty push in Sarajevo, the Great Foetus had not been born, his wife's death may have remained unconsummated for many, many years to come.

Still on the subject of births, Christmas 1913 was not a happy one for the Kitcheners. It is true that the spirit of the Nativity was touchingly reflected in the arrival of Edward and Louisa's second daughter on the 24th of December. Unfortunately, Alice, as she was duly christened, was born at 11:56 pm, an annoying four minutes short of the Grand Day. Her disconsolate father tried pleading 'slow clocks' in a doomed attempt to have the official registration of the birth amended. Tempting fate, Edward had predicted to all and sundry that the child would be born on Christmas Day. "If it's a boy we'll call it Christopha, an'," sticking out his chest with pride as he prepares to reveal his little gem, "if it's a girl we'll call it Mary Christmas!" To erase the disappointing memory, they called Alice Alice, which also happened to be the name of Louisa's overjoyed mother.

But that was not the end of it. Once tempted, fate seems to take a disproportionate number of reprisals, for not only had Edward been subjected to the agonies of the so-near-yet-so-far syndrome, but Alice, despite being born unprematurely, weighed in at a mere four pounds. Although she was in no danger, she would clearly require more care and attention than she might otherwise have done. The same could equally be said of her mother, who had haemorrhaged badly during the birth.

"You Jack, guv?"

"Tha's righ'."

A ragged boy hands him an envelope. "Lady says it's yer Christmas presen'."

"*Wha'* lady?" The boy darts off. "Oi!"

Jack rips open the envelope and pulls out a pink, painfully familiar handkerchief that reeks of stale sweat.

Much to the delight of everyone under the age of thirteen or so, the black Christmas of 1913 (as far as the Kitcheners were concerned) was also a white one. A very white one. The snow fell steadily from the first to the last day of the month. Yet Kilburn, like any other built-up area in the country, was not a Christmas-card picture of beauty. The endless columns of smoke rising into the leaden clouds like supportive pillars ensured that when it snowed, it snowed soot. Samuel Fox, a poet of the day, said, in an unpublished letter to *The Times*: "Penetrated like common harlots by the grime hurled heavenwards by our modern cities, how can the snows that virgin fell, virgin fall?"

Not since a May sky had looked down upon it with enviable indifference had High Road Kilburn been so congested with motor cars. Axle-deep in contaminated snow, a frozen herd of abandoned horse power waited patiently for the thaw that would

set it free. Consequently, the mighty hackney enjoyed a temporary revival. With their natural anti-freeze agents, they trotted
through the city's icy streets unperturbed and with restored dig-
nity. Swayed by such an encouraging sight, some ex-carmen
returned to the reins only to see their aspirations and renewed
trade melt away with the snow.

The makeshift museums of cars in the high road provided
the children of Kilburn with the perfect Christmas present.
Much to the annoyance of the vehicles' owners and a powerless
constabulary, the youngsters would spend most of the arctic day
climbing in and out of stranded automobiles. Claxons were hoot-
ed; steering wheels steered; gears engaged; handbrakes released.
To their credit, there was not a single instance of vandalism. This
was probably due to the fact that while the legal custodians of
the cars were not held in high esteem, their property most certainly was. The rich tones of the dashboard; the imposing authority of the speedometer; the sweet scent of soft, shiny leather
...these and other magical attributes combined to produce the
perfect insurance policy against damage. However, the adults of
Kilburn were unaware of the existence of such a policy, and often
took it upon their good selves to wave a chastising finger at the
high road pirates. Mr Laurence was no exception, which is why
Frankie broke his arm on the eve of Christmas Eve. The two were
trudging through the slush (outings of this nature were not
prohibited by the Elisabethan Carta) when Mr Laurence spotted
a couple of 'ruffians' driving along an imaginary thoroughfare
in a stationary Silver Ghost. For a man who had once, with some
pride, told his future in-law that the English were and had always
been a nation of explorers, he seemed wholly unaware of the
inestimable contribution that unbridled curiosity had made to
the cause of discovery. No slouch when it came to finger wagging,
Mr Laurence immediately raised his right arm, whereupon
Frankie, who had taken its stabilising presence into account when
calculating the minutiae of weight distribution, slid on the ice
and tumbled to the ground. For a few terrifying moments, he
lay motionless, his left arm folded under him. Then came the
first sighs of wincing pain, and the first in a torrent of cries. Mr
Laurence, like everyone else on the scene, stared at the boy with
wide-mouthed horror. "Don' move 'im!" shouted a voice from

the back of what had rapidly swelled into a crowd. All faces turned to its source. "Cummon, stan' back," ordered the man, forcing his way to Frankie's side. "He slipped," Mr Laurence told him by way of an explanation-cum-self-absolution. The man, whose sole credential was his air of authority, turned to the confectioner and asked if he was the boy's father. "I'm his guardian," was his reply, and he was suddenly all too aware of the damning incompatibility of that word and the pathetic spectacle of a prostrate, wailing child. "Give us yer tie," instructed the man. "Looks to me like 'e's broken 'is arm. I'll strap it up so you can take 'im to the bone-set'er." Mr Laurence's spine had never stooped with such gratitude. Hours later, though, it would stoop just as impressively (this time, with apologetic regret) when breaking the news of the broken arm to his wife.

To cap it all, the maternal head of the Kitchener clan almost became its deceased head on Christmas Eve. An obviously still displeased fate decreed that tragedy should strike when she was busy preparing the festive turkey (the other Turkey had been carved up the previous year). At first, Lady thought nothing of the insignificant scratch she received while grating breadcrumbs for the stuffing mixture. Three quarters of an hour later, the tip of her index finger had swollen to the size of a large marble. Worse still, the throbbing pain had spread to her arm.

A measure of the injury's gravity was Lady's decision to visit the local doctor. She regarded hippocratic oath-takers with contempt, often likening them to bloodthirsty butchers. Mary, who had recently followed in her elder sister's footsteps by joining the domestic ranks (she was serving in the very same Marshall regiment in Kensal Rise), accompanied her mother to Dr Gibbons' house. When he saw the inflamed finger-hand-arm, the doctor had to draw on all his professional expertise to disguise his deep concern. Indeed, as Elisabeth had done with Rose, Dr Gibbons remained calm and comforting.

"There's really nothing to worry about, Mrs Kitchener..."
"But, Doctor, look at my hand...my arm..."
"Yes, I can..."
"I can hardly move it!"
"You see..." He paused, but the layman's terms failed to

materialise inside his domed forehead. "The problem with septicaemia..."

"You can die from that, can't you, Doctor?"

"Oh, only in the most extreme cases. Now, please, you mustn't
fret like this. Septicaemia is produced by the presence of patho-
genic...that's disease-causing bacteria, in the blood. In some
cases, that can lead to serious disorders, *but in others*," responding
to the blank-faced terror on the faces opposite him, "the body,
left to its own devices, copes very well... Let's leave it another
hour or two. If the swelling hasn't shown signs of improvement
in that time then...well, we'll cross that bridge when and if we
come to it."

Word of the unfortunate incident spread from family member
to member as fast, if not faster, than the original spread of toxins
in Lady's fingertip. Loyal fledglings that they all were, each and
every one of them flocked to her side (excluding Edward, whose
wife was in the uncomfortable process of proving his yuletide
prediction wrong). Partially immersed in a saline solution, the
joint head of the family assured them all à-la-Gibbons that there
was really nothing to worry about. The afflicted limb informed
them otherwise as it carried on swelling like a balloon. At one
stage, when even the abandoned turkey was overshadowed by
its size, the arm seemed ripe for bursting.

Frank Kitchener could stand the idle waiting no longer. He
was a man who regarded illness and disease with the same kind
of contempt that his wife normally reserved for the medical profession. He pulled open a kitchen drawer and lit the stove. The
others were so preoccupied with the marrowlike arm that it came
as rather a shock to them when, minutes later, he approached
his wife holding a red-hot knife. "Le's 'ave yer 'and," he said
quietly. Lady stared into his steely eyes, and something in them
made her acquiesce to his demand. But the rest of the family,
who could see only a fuming blade inching towards a bloated
hand, rose to their feet shouting, "Dad!" with a single voice.
Breaths were held; eyes averted as the knife made contact with
the puffy end of her finger. One acute gasp later, hot water
turned red then a sickly shade of mauve as thick pus began ooz-
ing from the cut. Possessed by an overwhelming conviction that

he was doing the right thing, Frank assisted the golden exodus by applying gentle pressure along the length of Lady's arm. Slowly but surely, the swelling was going down and the pain subsiding. "Wha' yer need now's a little dram," and he went to a small cabinet which he always kept locked.

"You all righ', Mum?" asked Mary, looking very pale.

"I think so!" came the astonished reply.

And so it was that the air of an out-patient's waiting room infiltrated the traditional Christmas Day get-together at the senior Kitchener's residence in Keslake Road. There was an arm in a sling; a bandaged hand; a convalescent mother who had insisted on being present; an underweight baby; an eleven-month old sister gangrenous with jealousy; a mortified widower, and a father nursing a bilious grudge against the supernatural powers-that-be which had cheated him out of a "Mary Christmas".

No one, with the possible exception of a former carman, was sorry to see the back of 1913. Had they been blessed with Miss Dill's prescient talents, their attitude might well have been different.

Four

1914 commenced as promisingly for Mr Laurence in matters financial as it would end unpromisingly. In January of that year, the Manufacturing Confectioner's Alliance Company Ltd forced Mr Gerald Arthur John Kelly to close his shop on the grounds of bankruptcy. And even though the shop in question was at the opposite end of the high road, and despite feelings of genuine sympathy, Mr Laurence found it hard to resist the temptation to rub his hands in competitive glee. Someone's loss was always someone else's gain. The master's fractured ulna was a case in point. Had it not been a numismatic blessing in disguise for him, and a loss for Mr Bright, the piano teacher?

With these two gains very much in mind (and possibly to appease his conscience and impress his wife), Mr Laurence announced that Jack's earnings were to be incremented by 1/6 a week. Elisabeth, who, in the wake of the broken-arm-leading-to-the-suspension-of-piano-lessons, had decided to reinstate her daily literature classes, greeted the increase warmly. In fact, so gladdened was she by the news, that for a few days the strange heaviness that seemed to weigh her down vanished completely. Poor Mr Laurence! If only he could have afforded to raise Jack's wages every week. Predictably, when the uplifting effects of the pay-rise had worn off, her sombre mood returned.

Jack, who happened to be the most directly-affected party, received the news with an indifference that might easily have been misconstrued as the height of rudeness. But it had not escaped the notice of the Laurences that he had taken a decided turn for the worse since the bizarre delivery of an old handkerchief a few weeks earlier. Yet even prior to this, although he would never have admitted it, his state of mind, which continued to be a much-discussed topic in the family, had fractionally deteriorated as a result of Fred's fixation with Agatha. As much as he enjoyed the vivid accounts of their haystack frolics, a very bruised and vulnerable part of him could not help regarding the young maid as a threat to their cosy camaraderie. Jack reacted to these unmentionable feelings as he normally reacted: by withdrawing more and more into himself. Typically, Fred was far too busy recounting his latest exploits to detect any change in his friend.

The spirits in the bottle have worked their magic, and it is time to settle a score.

The street is all but deserted. Soiled slush is crispened by the cold of night. A man lurks in a doorway. Lights are extinguished, and he crosses the road. When he is about to knock on the door, another man steps out of an alleyway and calls to him.

"'Ere, cop 'ol' o'this!"

A piece of paper is thrust in his hand.

"Wha's this?"

"Sshhh! Can'cher see? It's a cheque. Look, it's signed by Taffy 'imself – see? David Lloyd George. It's worth thir'y bob. It's yours for a penny." The so-called cheque is handed back. "Cummon, don' be like tha'! It's a one-off!"

"Scarper!"

"All righ', but yer don' know wha'cher throwin' away."

"I said..."

"All righ', all righ', I'm goin'."

He waits for the young spiv to go, turns up the lapels of his coat then raps one of the glass panels in the door with his knuckles. When this elicits no response, he knocks more sternly and rattles the bolted door. "We're shut!" The voice is a distant one, so he keeps on rattling the door until he hears footsteps approaching on the other side of it. "Wha' is it?" "Impor'an' message for yer. Open up." "This time o'night? You mus' be barmy! Ge' lost!" He kicks the door hard. "Wha' d'yer think yer doin'?" "I got a message for yer from a frien' o'yours." Two eyes peer through the flowery design etched on the glass. "An' wha' frien' would tha' be?" "Didn' say 'is name." "Shove it under the door." "Can' – it ain' tha' kinder message." The door is unbolted, and he pushes his way into the stale penumbra. The lapels fall away from his face and she retreats a few steps, dragging her feet through the sawdust.

"Jack!"

He glares at her.

"Wha' d'yer wan'?"

"You shouldn've done wha' you did."

She retreats several more steps. "Tha' was jus' a joke."

"Call tha' a joke?"

"It was jus' sour grapes, tha's all. Wha' say we 'ave a drink, eh?"

Interpreting his silence as tacit agreement, she turns towards the bar. A hand grabs her arm and she lets out a shriek. "When did the penny drop, Moll?"

The alcohol on his breath does not bode well. "I'm really sorry, Jack! Please don' 'urt me!"

She is cowering, fearing the worst.

"You never wouldda sen' it if you 'adn' realised it mustta belonged ter..."

"Oi, mister, le' go of me mum!"

Jack spins round to see a young girl in a grubby night-dress.

"Vicky, ge' back up those stairs!" cries her mother.

"I wasn' gonna 'urt 'er," Jack assures the child, releasing Moll's arm.

"Oo is 'e, Mum?"

He stares from one to the other with an aggrieved expression flecked pathetically with shame and regret. Slowly, he turns his back on them and walks out.

"Oo was 'e, Mum?"

"Never you mine. 'E won' ever be comin' back, tha's all tha' mat'ers."

Following the birth of Alice Eloisa Kitchener, Elisabeth and Louisa saw a great deal more of each other. Elisabeth paid daily visits to her home in Kempe Road. Often, she would return to Kilburn with Lottie, a gesture much appreciated by Louisa. Alice's arrival had brought out the worst in the child. Reeling from the awful fact that she was no longer the most beautiful, most loved creature in the entire world, her frequent tantrums and moody silences had pushed a convalescing Louisa to the end of her tether. "I fel' like stranglin' 'er the other day," she once confided. "She jus' wouldn' stop screamin' so I 'it 'er. The little so-an'-so stared at me cool as yer like, run up t'our bedroom an' woke Alice up. Course, she star'ed bawlin' 'er eyes out – an' I'd jus' got 'er off t'sleep!"

Proving yet again that someone's loss is definitely someone else's gain, the temporary break in diplomatic relations between Louisa and her eldest daughter enabled her to concentrate on the pressing needs of her youngest. Of relatively less importance was the fact that Frankie inherited a near-constant playing companion during the month of January. Indeed, his one-year old cousin spent many a night at the house above the sweet shop. This short-lived treat pleased him no end, particularly since it seriously disrupted Elisabeth's attempts to read to him.

To the relief of everyone over the tender age of two and a half, Alice was scaling in at virtually normal weight come February. A couple of weeks later, she, Lottie, and her mother, accompanied by her aunt and cousin, made their first visit to the recently-opened King's Picture Palace in nearby Bannister Road.

At least on the face of it, things were getting back to normal.

A life as innocent as that which had inadvertantly plunged Lottie into misery was about to produce a similarly disturbing effect on her uncle Jack – the last thing his already fragile state of mind needed.

Playing with fire is a hazardous business. Putting it out, however, can be just as risky. The esoteric smoke that sealed a certain relationship was a natural symbol of the fate that would befall those concerned, for there is never any smoke without fire. Inside the shed; behind it, or in the stables, their passionate encounters were fiery, sizzling and steamy. In these unbearably torrid conditions, clothes were naturally cast off, and refreshing waters feverishly and athletically sought, for they could always be relied on to bring about a blissful extinction. Sadly, on one ill-fated occasion in the spring, the burning pyre was doused with waters of such infinite richness, that having extinguished the wild flames (as Jack had been managing to do in the safety of his dreams), they proceeded to irrigate what proved to be a treacherously-fertile soil. The subsequent extinction of the fruit that duly flourished was once again feverishly sought, yet anything but blissful.

"Jacko! Ya've gotta 'elp me," a collarless Fred pleads.

Nervously, he wipes away the perspiration on the back of his neck. As is their usual, evening custom, both men are at the kitchen table. Auburn curls of tobacco lie between them.

"Is she sure?"

"Yeah...regular as clockwork she is. If 'er paren's fine out they'll kill bofe of us, an' if Blishen fines out we'll be out on our ears. She's gotta 'ave one soon, Jacko! Before it star's t'show."

"Fred...you should've been more careful."

"Course I should've – goes withou' sayin' – but tha' kiner talk's no good t'me now, is it? The 'orse 'as already bol'ed."

"It was boun' t'appen. Any'ow, I think there's someone who can 'elp, but for God's sake, Fred, don' lerrit 'appen again."

"It won', Jacko – hones' t'God. 'Sides, it's all over between us."

With a look of resigned determination; the faintest of emotional warning bells already ringing in his ears, Jack gets to his feet. Donning his overcoat, he advises his friend to keep his heavily-nicotined fingers crossed.

The young man who has just been invited to sit down radiates a disconcerting air of confidence. Young men in frayed coats and cracked boots should not be so at ease. Predictably, his incongruous composure has placed everyone on their guard. Like tennis spectators, the eyes of the assembled members of the host family (but none more so than Mary's) flit from seated youth to seated parents.

"'Ow's yer 'and now, Mrs Kitchener? Mary tol' me all abou' it."

"Much better, thank you."

"Same kinder fing 'appened to me aunt Lil as it 'appens, only she wasn' so lucky. They 'ad ter chop it off inner end. Didn' do 'er any good, though, cos she curled up 'er toes wivin a week."

The flitting eyes are stationary. Anxiously, they await the tell-tale signs that soon (oh no!) surface on parental faces.

"Mary tells us you've no job at the..."

"Tha's righ'. Still, it ain' the ender the world, is it?"

"Wha'cher mean, it ain' the ender the world!" shouts Frank, leaning forward. Mary turns away.

"I mean there's ways an' there's means."

"An' wha's tha' supposed t'mean?"

"It means there's no need for yer t'worry. I'll take care of 'er all righ'."

"Over my dead body you will."

It is game, set and match to the older generation. Mary rushes out of the room. Whispering teenagers confirm to one another that her young man's crushing defeat has brought tears to her eyes.

Her vanquished but evidently unbowed suitor raises a nonchalant eyebrow as he gets calmly to his feet. "Guess I'd bet'er be on me way, then. Can' say it's been a pleasure, bu' you can' win 'em all, can yer?"

"I'm expecting her back any minute. Would you care to come in?" says the extremely gaunt man at the door.

"Er, yes, thank you."

"I expect it's about a happy event. It usually is."

Jack nods and follows the man into the house, where he is ushered into a small, firelit room.

"There we are, do make yourself at home, Mr...?"

"Kitchener. You sure I ain' inconveniencin' yer?"

"No, not at all. She'll be back in a jiffy... I was just about to pour myself a cup of tea. Would you..."

"No thank you. I 'ad some before comin' ou'."

Jack warms his hands by the fire.

"How about a drop of sherry to warm you up?"

The hospitality of the thin man (not unlike the confidence of the young man) is disturbing. Jack had wanted to get the whole, sordid affair over and done with as quickly as possible. Before seizing the awesome brass lion on the front door he had taken a deep breath. The last thing he wanted was to be made a fuss of by someone who doubtless thought him a prospective father.

"No thank you."

"It's perishing cold for this time of year, isn't it?"

"Yes," he replies, struggling to sound enthusiastic.

Mercifully, the man desists from offering him anything else, and leaves Jack on his own. A large clock on the mantelpiece noisily marks the demise of each second. In the presence of a single, muted human, it has taken centre stage. Confirming the subservient nature of the relationship, Jack begins pacing the room in strict time.

The clock's spell is abruptly broken by the sound of the front door opening and closing. Stopped in his tracks, he hears voices in the corridor outside. Then footsteps. Butterflies stir within as, heralded by creaking floorboards, a heavily-built woman enters the room.

"Mr Kitchener, how are we?"

"Very well, thank you. Mrs Bowman, I 'ope I ain'...."

"And how's the little one coming on?"

"Oh, 'e's growin' by the secon'."

"And what about you, Mr Kitchener – how are you coping?"

Why is it that the last things that people want are all too often the first on other people's list of priorities? "Oh, I can' complain. I, er...wan'ed ter...there's something I wonna talk to yer abou'."

"Oh?"

Jack casts a nervous glance at Mr Bowman, whom he has just noticed standing partially eclipsed in the doorway. "It's...a personal mat'er."

"Ah, yes, of course." The gaunt man shuffles uneasily on his feet. "I'll be in the kitchen if anyone needs me."

Mrs Bowman closes the door and turns inquiringly to Jack.

"A frien' of mine – a good frien', 'e lives with me, 'as got this girl, where 'e works, inter trouble... She's only sixteen, an' if 'er paren's fine ou' they'll kill 'er, so...well, there's jus' one thin' they can do...an' I was wonderin' if..."

"I'm sorry, but that is quite out of the question. My job is to deliver God's children, not... I don't have anything to do with that sort of thing."

Mrs Bowman's flat refusal puts paid to the awkward niceties that have stifled him thus far. "But she's desperate. If you don' do it she'll 'ave it done by some butcher you wouldn' trus' with yer dog...She's only sixteen, Mrs Bowman – an' scared ou' of 'er wits."

"But you don't realise what it is you're asking me to do."

Her resolve is clearly flagging. "I'm askin' yer t'save a girl's life...'er future... Without yer 'elp, we could end up losin' both of 'em."

"How pregnant is she?" The question is a resigned sigh.

"She's only jus' foun' ou', so it can' be long."

"I don't know, Mr Kitchener...one has principles." Another resigned sigh. "But to forsake that poor, frightened girl..."

A forlorn-looking figure encased in a black coat turned left into an Eresby Road that had long ago ceased smelling of dead dog. She walked briskly, staring at her shadow on the early morning frost. Viewed from a first floor window, bonnetted and red-cheeked, she seemed even younger than she was.

Jack alighted the stairs two steps at a time and opened the door.

"Cold, innit?" he said cheerfully, then cursed himself for sounding just like Mr Bowman.

"Yes," replied the girl quietly.

"It's up 'ere," said Jack, motioning to the staircase.

As they made their way up, he felt a sudden pang of compassion for the "poor, frightened girl" ahead of him. The imagined threat to his chummy relationship with Fred, whom he had so resented in the abstract, was nothing more than a nervous, frail-looking adolescent straining visibly to hold back the tears. His heart went out to her, and although he had never admitted it to himself, the conviction that he had somehow wronged her came to the fore of his emotions. At the top of the stairs, Jack placed his hand gently on her arm, "You sure you wonna go through with this, luv?" She stared up at him as though he had spoken in a foreign language. He was about to repeat the question when her small lips parted as if she were about to yawn, and tears rolled down her face from narrowed eyes. Sobbing inconsolably, she bowed her head and sought refuge in his fatherly arms. Jack raised his eyes to the flaking ceiling, and wondered what on earth he had got himself into. Patting her on the back with one hand, he searched for a handkerchief with the other. "'Ere y'are, luv, 'ave a good blow." Agatha did as she was told.

"I'm so scared!"

"Mrs Bowman'll be 'ere any minute. If yer wonna change yer... Le's go inside, any'ow."

The girl made straight for the fireplace. "Me mum an' dad would kill me if they knew abou' this."

Jack felt haunted by those words. They had been used to entice him into helping, and he, in turn, had used them to persuade Mrs Bowman. He sunk his hands deep into his pockets and walked across the room to the window overlooking the road.

"Is tha' where 'e sleeps?" asked Agatha, staring at the rectangular length of timber screwed to the wall.

"Yes...it's collapsable."

"I know, 'e's always goin' on abou' it."

"She's 'ere," he announced, his voice charged with urgency. "Well?"

The young maid stared at him entreatingly for a few moments, as if awaiting some sort of sign. Then, averting her wistful gaze, she began unfastening the strings of her bonnet with exaggerated care. After exchanging one final, mournful look with him, she turned and set about the buttons of her coat with increasing haste.

Jack went to open the door.

It was the stuff of burgeoning martyrdom. Sweeping aside all personal and professional considerations, Elisabeth had accepted a poor, motherless child as her own; she had then gone on to marry a parabolic sweet-seller out of expediency, not love; she had been 'Libbified', and she had been forced to replace one Lear with another Lear's *Book of Nonsense* – all this without a single murmur of complaint to anyone.

No, quite clearly, the Ecce Homo was more, far more, than just a symbol of the copulative sacrifice carried out beneath it with ever-decreasing regularity. Unlike Louisa, who would have buried the lurid image in the trunk where she had once unearthed the photograph of a bogus mistress, Elisabeth, perhaps intuiting its sacrificial relevance to virtually all aspects of her life, had grown fonder and fonder of it. The natural outcome of this unspoken affinity with the crucified man was her eventual acquisition of a small wooden cross on a silver chain. At first, the gibbet was discreetly concealed under blouses or carefully-pinned neckerchiefs, but it wasn't long, however, before she was wearing it quite openly – and it was to dangle, for all to see, in the valley of two modest golgothas until her dying day.

The fall shakes the whole house. Jack runs to the door and down the stairs recalling a similar incident in a public house he would prefer *not* to recall. As then, Fred reeks of alcohol. Blood trickles from his nose. "Fred!" Drunken groans spill out of him when he is shaken. "Fred! Gerrup!" It is asking too much of the sprawling body – it must be hauled up the steep ascent and into the privacy of their lodgings. It is back-breaking work, and by the time Jack reaches his landing and drags his load through the door of their flat, he is soaked in sweat and gasping for breath. After dumping Fred on the floor, he makes straight for the water basin, peels off his shirt, and sloshes handfuls of water over his head, nape, shoulders. Without bothering to towel himself down, he fills up a pitcher and empties it over the snoring drunk.

"Wha' the bleedin' 'ell... Jacko, ol' son!" He tries to stand up, but his rubbery legs send him crashing back to the floor. "Blimey, must've 'ad one too many."

"You oughtta be ashamed of yerself!"

Jack is standing over him, still holding the pitcher.

"Ashamed!" repeats Fred, rummaging through his pockets. "Why should I shame afeeled...I mean...Ah, 'ere it is! I go' us a lit'le somink t'celebrate – see?" Jack grabs the bottle and sends it skimming across the floor of the room. "'Ere, wha's go' inter yer?"

Seizing him by the lapels of his coat, he yanks Fred towards him. "Don' you ever make me go through anythin' like this mornin' again!"

Fred, his hair parted down the middle by the water, stares at him wondering what on earth he has done wrong. Jack had willingly arranged everything, hadn't he? So wha's the problem?

Why don' Jacko wonna celebra'e now the worst's over? Wha' 'e needs' a drink t'soften 'im up a bit. He drags himself in the direction of the discarded bottle, but Jack beats him to it.

"'Aven' you 'ad enough?" He uncorks the bottle and pours its contents down the sink.

"Jacko, no!" Fred closes his eyes, devastated. "Why d'yer go an' do tha' for? I go' it so we could celebra'e."

"Celebra'e! Yes, Fred, le's celebra'e. Le's drink t'Agatha, shall we? To yer darlin' Agatha! Le's toas' to the way she screamed 'er 'ead off this mornin', eh?...to the way she jus' lay there afterwards all pale an' still...on the same bed where Rose died in me arms..."

Fred's head slumps shamefully to the floor. Pulling on a clean shirt, Jack ignores the slurred apologies, dons his overcoat and leaves the room, slamming the door behind him (you can 'ear a pin drop when those two's in).

It was late. More to the point, *he* was late. Jack crossed the high road and broke into a rhythmic canter. By the time he reached the bottom of Victoria Road, he was nauseously out of breath and sweating profusely again. He walked the rest of the way to the Falcon Hotel, where Mary and her young man had arranged to meet him.

"Though' you wasn' comin'," said Mary after he had bought himself a pint of stout and joined them in a smoky recess of the busy bar.

"I 'ad ter sor' somethin' ou' with Fred."

"I can' stay much longer cos mum an' dad'll star' fret'in'. This is Billy." The two men nodded to each other. There was something vaguely familiar... "Jack, we wonna ge' married."

"Wha's the 'urry?" Yes, there was definitely something about the young man in the frayed overcoat and cracked boots that seemed vaguely...

"We've made up our mines. We...love each other, Jack, an'...I don' 'ave ter tell yer wha' it's like t'be in love."

Jack bit his lip, and then glanced at the youth as though curious to determine what it was that his sister had seen in him. "You ain' tol' mum and dad this, 'ave yer?"

"Course no'. They won' even le' us see each other – but if you talked to 'em, Jack...they'd listen t'yer, I know they would." The frown on Jack's face was not very encouraging. "Oh I 'ate 'em! They're actin' jus' like they did when Libby wannid t'marry Ernest."

"Wha' sor' of work d'yer do, Billy?"

"I'm lookin' fer a job, as it 'appens."

"Don' I know you from someplace?" asked Jack, staring him in the eye.

"Don' fink so."

"Will yer talk to 'em Jack?" intervened Mary.

"The thin' is...withou' a job..."

"You foun' Fred one, didn' yer. Maybe you could..."

"Fred's got a trade, Mary – 'as Billy?"

She lowered her gaze and turned deflatedly to the young man. He, in turn, put on a brave face and said, chirpily, "Somefink's boun' t'come up soon."

Unimpressed by this, Jack sipped his beer with a stony expression.

"I've go' t'get back now," said Mary, despondently.

"I'll...see wha' I can do," Jack tried to reassure her.

Her face lit up and she gave his hand an affectionate squeeze – but what could he possibly say to his parents? he wondered as the pair of them inched their way to the door. He couldn't very well tell them that they were wrong to be concerned about their daughter's future. Jobs were hard to come by. How could they possibly make ends meet on her paltry earnings? He downed the rest of the beer and shut his eyes. It had been a long, draining day. So much to ponder over: that poor girl...Fred...Mary and her young man – her young man who looked so familiar...

The background buzz of voices filtering gently through the haze afforded him by the stout, began lulling him into a pleasant, trancelike state. He was about to fade out of consciousness altogether when a single, drifting word jolted him back to reality: 'Taffy', and from the reality of the bar it sent his mind spiralling to a shadowy doorway and a counterfeit cheque...*see? David Lloyd George. It's worth thir'y bob. It's yours for a penny.* Clenching his fists, Jack made a dash for the exit. The long, draining day was far from over.

Running as fast as he could, he caught sight of them on the corner of Milman Road. They were in each other's arms and pressed against the railings of Queen's Park. Careful not to be spotted, Jack waited at a distance, his gaze focusing discreetly on the dark, open spaces of the park rather than on the lovers' embrace. After a while, they set off hand in hand, and just as Jack had anticipated, they kissed each other goodbye on the corner of Keslake Road. Billy retraced his steps until he found Jack blocking his path.

"Jack, wha' yer doin' 'ere?"

"You're a spiv, Billy."

"Wha' yer talkin' abou'?"

"You migh' no' remember me, bu' I remember you."

"You're mixin' me up with someone else."

"Ou'side the Cock, remember? You tried sellin' me one of Taffy's cheques."

"Tha' was never you, was it?" Billy tilts his head to the heavens and lets out a long, incredulous sigh. "All righ', but tha's go' nuffink to do with me an' Mary."

"It's go' *everythin'* t'do with you an' Mary, cos if you think we're gonna stan' by an' le' a nice, decen' girl like *'er* get mixed up with the likes of you, you've got anuvver thin' comin'."

Once again, the young man turns to the heavens. How can he make these thick-skulled Kitcheners understand that spiv or no spiv, his feelings for Mary are completely legitimate?

"All righ', le' me ge' this straigh'. Wha' yer wan' is tha' I never see 'er again, righ'?"

"Righ'."

"She'll miss me like mad."

"No' when I tell 'er the truth abou' yer, she won'."

"She'll 'ate yer for it," he prophesies with his more customary nonchalance.

The Great Foetus is almost upon us. The snows of Christmas and the unseasonable cold of the early spring months seem but a far-off memory. Temperatures have gradually risen, days gradually lengthened. And arms that were fractured and septic are healthy again.

It is Wednesday, the 24th of June, 1914, and there are three candles reflected in the eyes of a proudly-gathered clan. A small boy extinguishes them *and* his mounting excitement with his second mighty puff (a much more sensible way of quelling one's feverish emotions), and everybody cheers.

It is Sunday, the 28th of June, 1914, and there is burning rubble reflected in the eyes of a proudly-gathered crowd. Master Nedjelko's explosive attempt to quell *his* fiery passions has failed. Everybody cheers... Forty-five minutes later, in that very same part of the Austro-Hungarian Empire, a triumphant Archduke Francis Ferdinand, heir-presumptive to the Austrian throne, and his morganatic wife Sophie enjoy the festive air as they drive through the thronging streets of Sarajevo. Gavrilo Princip breathes in the heady atmosphere, and his pulse begins to race. It will require more than a mighty puff or two to satisfy *him*. Caressing a clandestine shaft, the young student soon reaches a deadly point of no return. Intoxicated; eyes fully dilated; his heart pounding pounding pounding, he surges forward. Heads turn. There are shouts; screams – but it is too late. His glistening barrel recoils with blissful power once twice thrice...

Take your seats, everyone! No, not in the gory, stomach-turning operating theatre. The fiendish labour is over. The offensive pushing has ceased. The monster has been safely delivered. No...we are about to enter the absurd theatre of war.

Five

As far as the eye can see there are erect forefingers pointing
patriotically. Fifty-four million of them. They protrude two-
dimensionally from the base of Nelson's heroic pillar; from the
sides of omnibuses and trams; from every hoarding and from
every window. Below each foreshortened digit are the following
words: "Join your country's army! God save the King." And
something quite extraordinary begins to happen. It can only be
appreciated fully from a great height – a height so great, in fact,
that as we peer down on a nation that now seems no larger
than...well, than a chessboard, the only detectable sign of human
life is not the glint on a king's crown or a bishop's chalice or a
knight's shining armour – it is the hundreds upon hundreds of
tiny eddies of dustlike particles, each and every one of them
conforming to a swirling pattern which resembles the behaviour
of iron filings around the pole of a magnet. Drawing closer to
the ground, the 'iron filings' turn out to be hordes of young,
gallant men, and only then do we see that the mobilising 'magnet' is none other than the Great, Mass-Produced Finger itself.
Its pulling power can already be felt on the beaches of France,
where...but no, the infectious patriotic fervour, not to mention
the light-headedness induced by our abrupt ascent into the
heavens, has made us get ahead of ourselves. *Rewind*: soldiers
on Gallic shores speed backwards into vessels that sail for England preceded by a foaming surf. At Sheerness, large crowds
wave farewell to disembarking troops. Special trains bound for
Willesden Junction Station imbibe their own steam as they pull
out. Back in London, hundreds of relatives wait tearfully outside
the station as train after train reverse towards them. A Drum and

79

Fife band is on hand to escort the retreating volunteers via Harlesden back to the 9th Battalion Middlesex Territorial Regiment at Pound Lane. *Stop*.

The Show must go on, and so it did. Barely two days after Emperor Francis Joseph had declared war on Serbia, the Kilburn Grange Cinema and Winter Garden opened its majestic doors to the public for the first time. At precisely 8pm on the 30th of July, *She Stoops to Conquer* flickered onto a virgin screen. (Was the choice of film an arbitrary one, or could it possibly have had anything to do with the claim made by proud Kilburnians that Goldsmith wrote his famous work in a nearby farm, when the Bourne flowed freely and untainted, and Kilbourne was still renowned for its luscious tea gardens?) Among those fortunate enough to be present on that historic evening were Mr and Mrs Ernest V. Laurence, for whom a certain Mr Kitchener had unselfishly baby-sat. And while the first-night audience watched enthralled, loyal servants of the Crown worked behind the scenes preparing the Defence of the Realm Act (hereinafter called 'Dora'), whose dramatic powers were to eclipse even those of the great Miss Bernhardt.

With lights suitably dimmed, *The Great War* officially premièred on the 28th of July, 1914 (it would not open in Britain until the 4th of August). Boasting an impressive and ever-increasing cast of millions, and with the world literally as its stage, it would run for 1,567 nights, and tour no fewer than thirty-two nations. Yet even the best and biggest productions are not without their critics. Take, for instance, the Harlesden Freedom League, who immediately took it upon itself to condemn Britannia's protagonistic part in the war despite her longstanding contractual obligations. Its members, of course, soon got their much-deserved comeuppance. In an incident not dissimilar to the one spearheaded by Richard Annenberg in Messina Avenue, the self-appointed joy-killers were attacked by an angry crowd during a meeting held in Manor Park Road, proving once again that no one should ever underestimate the sensibilities of the discerning public at large.

Jack shuts the door behind him. There are no customers in

the shop. In fact, there are precious few customers in most of the high road shops. Everyone seems to have taken to the streets. Desperate for information, hundreds of people anxiously await the next newspaper edition. When it arrives, the copies are engulfed by a sea of hands, and after barely a few seconds, fresh snippets of news are rippling their way to those on the fringes of the crowd.

Mr Laurence, who until then had been hunched over his counter, looks up at him. "You didn't manage to get one, I see."

"No, it's bedlam out there! I've never seen so many people in me life."

Alerted by the shop bell, Elisabeth hurries down, preceded by Frankie.

"Any luck, Jack?"

"Daddy!" shouts the boy, bounding across the shop to his father.

"Too many people," he replies, tousling Frankie's hair. "Any-'ow, I did fine somethin' ou'. Some White'all people 'ave taken over the bus garages in Willesden an' Cricklewood, an' there's notices everywhere callin' up the Territorials."

"There's no turning back now," sighs a beetle-browed Mr Laurence. "It'll be conscription next."

"Oh Jack, is it really that serious? The thought of you all being called up..."

"Wha' cod up?" Frankie interrupts her, staring at his father.

Jack picks him up. "Oh, it's nothin' for lit'le uns like you to worry abou'." Turning to Elisabeth and her husband, he adds, "They reckon it's volun'eers they wan', thousan's of 'em."

"Volunteers?" echoes Mr Laurence with a reflex hunching of his back by a few extra degrees.

"Jack," says Elisabeth, detecting something in his look, "you're not thinking of enlisting, are you?"

"Well, me an' Fred 'ave sor' of made up our..."

"Oh Jack, no!"

"The war'll probably be over by the time they've trained us." His sister cannot conceal her anguish. "Probably be all over by nex' week."

With scant regard to repeated pleas by the authorities and

the press to "act as you always act", the same sea of hands that had engulfed each newspaper edition as it hit the streets, eventually surged into every available provisions shop, and swept away vast quantities of food. To safeguard dwindling stocks, traders doubled their prices. Not so, however, Mr Laurence, whose nectareous wares were sadly overlooked by the wave of panic-buyers. Unfortunately for him, someone else's loss of merchandise was exclusively their own gain.

But what matters individual loss in times of grave National Emergency? The Show must; has to; will, to the very end, go on. With this firmly in mind, Middlesex exhibitors who open on Sundays resolve to set up the Middlesex Cinema War Fund for the relief of local widows-to-be and their children. "Enlist Now!" The message is being projected loud and clear to audiences up and down Old England. Vitagraphs such as "Our Coast Defences", with its moving pictures of warships, accompanied by martial strains of military and naval music, provide the perfect, antidotal context to personal hardship. "I want you!" The response to this, as we have already witnessed from on high, is quite extraordinary. "Forward to Victory." The 'gigantic experiment' of the mustachioed Secretary of State for War is proving a resounding success. Who else but a renowned celibate would have dreamed of re-channelling his male vigour into a digital erection of such epic proportions? Now he, too, is a weaver of fictions, but his celebrated index finger is far, far from Sistine-like. "Is your best boy wearing khaki?" The Ministry of War is swamped with hopeful auditioners – but they need not fear...there are parts for everybody. "Every fit man wanted." Huge queues of cloth-capped and bowler-hatted youths wait outside every recruiting office. "Rally round the flag." Distress committees empowered to formulate relief schemes mushroom in the patriotic downpour. And slowly, as sanity prevails, the panic-buyers stop panicking...stocks accumulate...prices fall..."God save the King" (not to mention the Pied Piper of Whitehall).

The nonchalant prophecy proved sadly accurate. When Mary was told the truth about her young man, she clenched her fists and screamed. It was a high-pitched scream, unnervingly consistent in both tone and volume. Her brothers and parents listened to the monotonous, shrill cry in bewildered silence. When, in sheer desperation, her father slapped her across the face, she duly fainted. From that miserable day on, she only spoke to members of her family if pressed into doing so, and then only monosyllabically. She had sent herself to Coventry, and all of them to Hell.

As predicted, the main butt of her hatred was her brother Jack. She began writing him vitriolic letters in which he was accused of all manner of things. Her most obsessive accusation was that since losing Rose he could not abide the thought of anybody else having a loved one by their side. This, she insisted, was the sole reason why he had not objected to Elisabeth marrying Mr Laurence, "we all know it was a marriage of convenience". By the fourth missive, Jack gave up reading them. Angry, hurt and confused (as only he could be), he hurled them unopened into the fireplace.

Not a single member of the Kitchener family, related by blood or otherwise, could get through to her. A distraught Lady pleaded with Jack to find Billy ("Maybe we *have* been a little harsh"), but Billy was nowhere to be found, and the rift between them and Mary became a festering, open wound. Yet surely even a heart as broken as hers would warm with fraternal love at the sight of...

"Mary, love, there's someone to see you!"

"Wha'?"

"I said there's someone to see you... She's upstairs packing all her things. It saddens me to say it, but she can't wait to move in with the Marshalls. Mary, love!"

"Comin'!"

The sound of floorboards creaking under a weight that moves across them with melancholic abandon; the defiant expression on the face that appears in the doorway; the cold eyes that take in the blue serge jacket, khaki trousers, and boots.

"They've given us these jackets cos there ain' enough khaki t'go roun' yet," explains Jack with a forced grin. Lady studies her daughter's face, praying for the frost to melt. "They call it Kitchener blue, so all the lads keep takin' the mickey...They're a good bunch, though."

"Jack and the boys might have to go and fight those awful

Germans," remarks Lady, hurling another ember into the fire of reconciliation.

The face with the defiant expression and cold eyes withdraws from sight. The creaking abandon is no longer melancholic – it is decidedly gay. As a tearful mother is comforted by her heroic son, a voice chillingly devoid of all emotion wafts down the stairwell, through the hall and into the room.

"Good luck to 'em!"

The summer of 1914 was as warm and pleasant as the winter had been ruthlessly cold. Hot suns shone down endlessly from acres of clear, blue sky, and as the temperature rose, so did the fever of war. The Evil, Child-Bayoneting Hun was to be punished. The whole nation, awakened each dawn by the cock-a-doodle-doo of a sergeant-major, was alive with the vibrant sound of bugles ringing from every drill hall and park; with the sound of sun-kissed trains, Kitchener-blue arms waving from every window, cutting through the countryside like giant centipedes; with the sound of stirring speeches and rousing sermons; with the sound of national anthems, Rule Britannias and Tipperaries, and, most importantly, with the pious buzz that emanated from the knowledge that God was on their side (had not the Dalai Lama Himself offered King George one thousand of his troops?).

It was a committed nation at arms in which, overnight, two purulent specimens of life had hatched into existence: the Alien and the Shirker. The first of these, who went under such give-away names as Bernstein, Steineke, Stohwasser or Rosenhein, were obvious security risks, and had their every move monitored. Changing their names to Curzon, Stanley, Stowe or Rose only served to confirm their suspected status as undercover agents. This, however, could not be said of the good King, who, three years into the war, in an act as altruistic as it was patriotic, changed his family name from Saxe-Coburg-Gotha to Windsor. While First Sea Lords and Lord Chancellors with dubious surnames fell foul of an epidemic of whispering campaigns, the King left no one in any doubt as to where his own loyalties lay (not that there was a single subject in his entire kingdom who had ever entertained such doubts) by axing the German and Austrian emperors from the roll of Knights of the Garter. (It is extremely difficult to gauge the damage inflicted on each of the tyrants' morales by George V's momentous decision, and even harder to estimate the number of lives it ultimately saved.)

The second of these specimens was immeasurably more repugnant. The Shirker, also known as the Slacker, was the apostate precursor of the post-Somme, post-conscription Conscientious Objector. Unlike the Alien, he could not be monitored. Worse still, he could not be arrested and deported if he failed to take himself to his local police station at the time designated. No, the Shirker was the kind of anonymous creature who would rather serve a tennis ball than his country; who would rather be frolicking in the back row of a picture house than fighting on the front, and because of this, he posed as much risk to the security of his motherland as did the Evil Boche. His ears were congenitally deaf to the pleas of sweethearts, parents, and, most incredibly of all, Miss Gladys Morgan's moving rendition of Paul Reuben's "Your King and Country Need You"; his sense of shame untouched even by the award of white feathers by devoted young girls on the lookout for men still in civvies. In those times of grave National Emergency, the Slacker was nothing more or less than the most contemptible of life forms.

Baby Alice, whose ill-timed birth eight months earlier had shown that predictions were not always destined to be accurate, took her first tentative steps in the house above the sweet-shop. The event was witnessed by her proud mother and aunt as they sipped their afternoon tea. Frankie and Lottie, who were playing in the same room at the time, refused to attach any importance to the feat. After all, they had been performing it daily for as long as either of them could remember, and just to prove the point they began sprinting as fast as they could from one wall to another. The noise generated by all this activity was more than the novice walker could cope with, and she burst into tears.

"Never mind!" Louisa comforted her. "You *are* a clever girl, aren'cher?"

"Here, let me hold her," said Elisabeth.

"Go t'Auntie Libby? There we go."

As Louisa looked on, she could not help thinking how much her sister-in-law had aged recently. Her youthful complexion had lost much of its vitality, and fine lines now meandered under her eyes and the drooping tips of her mouth. Watching her nuzzle Alice with an affection of much greater intensity than that normally expressed by an aunt to a niece, Louisa reflected on how different things might have been had Elisabeth married a 'real' man. Nothing could compare with the weight of a strong, virile male pumping pelvically on top of you; filling you with his children. Young women needed young men. Like with like. Anything else was ungodly.

"Oh, quick, there must be a parade!" cried Elisabeth, rushing to the open window.

Distant drums and pipes were drawing nearer by the second. The large crowd gathered down below cheered with nervous anticipation.

"Where de soldures?" asked Frankie, craning his neck.

"They're coming, can't you hear them?" replied Elisabeth, who was still holding Alice with obvious relish.

With a triumphant increase in volume, the first men came into view, but much to the children's disappointment, they were clad in chequered skirts. The fact that these skirts were called 'kilts', and that the brave, marching recruits belonged to the London Scottish Regiment, did little to soften the blow. Luckily, no one else seemed to share their aversion to kilted troops. Union Jacks fluttering like a swarm of red, white and blue butterflies were to be seen everywhere; policemen on duty saluted them with unconcealed admiration; huge sheets with makeshift 'good luck' messages draped out of every other window. Eventually, and much to the delight of the unimpressed youngsters, "real soldures", in the shape of the Territorials, filed past. Although khaki was once again the predominant colour, many men still wore the blue jackets that paid colourful testimony to the success of the Secretary of State for War's recruiting campaign. As far as Frankie was concerned, though, every religiously-pointed-out man in blue was "Daddy". Predictably, Lottie began making similar claims, and when the pair of them happened to select the same private, Frankie became so incensed that he kicked his cousin in the leg. She elbowed him back, whereupon he kicked her again. This impromptu outbreak of hostilities resulted in Frankie being banished from the window.

"It's a real shame t'see 'em go," remarked Louisa later.

"I know, that's just how I felt when Jack enlisted. But it's at times like these one has to put those sorts of feelings aside. It's for a great cause, Louisa – we mustn't forget that."

"Yeah, bu' why should my Eddie an' others like 'im risk their lives over an ol' scrap of paper?"

"Because...a principle's at stake," explained Elisabeth, fingers tightening around her cross. "Like it or not, everyone has to stand up for what they believe is right."

"Well I still think it's a cryin' shame," insisted Louisa, ruefully reviewing the marching young men imprinted on her mind.

Pausing briefly, Elisabeth's own thoughts turned to another matter. "What *is* a shame is the way Mary's been behaving during all of this."

"I know, it's jus' not like 'er, is it?"

"Maybe it *is* just like her and none of us ever realised it... It pains me to say it, but I feel she's died as far as the family's concerned."

"Don' say tha'. She's boun' t'come to 'er senses one of these days – jus' you wai' an' see."

Elisabeth tugged at her cross, and lowered her voice until it was barely audible. "This mustn't go further than these four walls: she's been writing Jack some horrible letters."

"Ge' away!"

She nodded sombrely. "I was there tidying their rooms a few days ago when I noticed a pile of envelopes in the fireplace. 'Strange place to leave letters,' I thought, noticing that most of them were unopened and in Mary's hand. I know I shouldn't have, but I read a few of them and..."

"You didn'!"

"It was a shameful thing to do, I know, but something impelled me to. Well...I saw at once why Jack was intending to burn them." Louisa was now hanging on her every word with a frozen look of intrigued disbelief. "They could have been written by the Devil himself! In one of them, she says how glad Jack must be knowing I share my bed with a man like Ernest – her meaning is obvious."

"Is it?" asked Louisa, hoping for a graphic elucidation.

It was not forthcoming, though, and while she was sorely

tempted to use the opportunity to broach the subject once and for all of Elisabeth's evidently unhappy love-life, her nerve failed her and she added, tamely, "Wha' else does she say?"

"Well, in another letter, she writes about how much she still loves Billy; how she thinks about him every moment of the day – but especially at nights..."

"Go on."

"Oh, she's so cruel! She'll burn in hell for this."

"For *wha*'?"

The lover of Shakespeare, Byron and Keats gazed down at her lap guiltily. "She tells him how she lies awake at nights... touching herself...pretending it's... The girl's depraved, Louisa!"

"She's jus' love-sick, tha's all. It's an illness like any other, only there's no cure, well, no quick cure. Takes time. Not everyone's as strong as you are, you know."

"Oh I hope you're right, and that one day, in spite of everything, I'll find it in my heart to forgive her."

"If anyone can, you can."

At that precise moment, the door opened, and in walked Mr Laurence. He was carrying small bags of sweets for each of the children. Noticing that baby Alice was walking unaided across the room, he cried, "Well done, Alice!", causing the infant to falter and fall back onto her padded rump.

"You startled the poor darling!" snapped his wife. "The last thing we want is another broken arm."

Yes, thought Louisa as, smiling awkwardly at Mr Laurence, she picked up her daughter: it must be a *very* unhappy love-life.

The jubilantly-received declaration of war could not have come at a better time for Fred. The regrettable incident with Agatha had marred both his working hours at the Blishen household and his hours of leisure at his own abode, where his living companion had grown embittered with life in general as swiftly as he had with him in particular. Efforts to patch things up between them failed miserably, and as if to emphasize the extent of the rift, Jack gave up smoking and Charlton Athletic. By the time those mysterious letters began piling up in the hearth, the Trappist withdrawal into himself was all but complete. For Fred, there was no longer anything interesting to do at home, so, not surprisingly, the lure of the public house became increasingly difficult to resist. And it was then, as debauched gaiety beckoned, that a scrap of paper was violated, a principle upheld, and a nation called to arms. Not a moment too soon, the past was on the verge of becoming a thing of the past. Here was an historic opportunity to begin anew, to burn the temporal bridges, to march forward towards personal and collective glory. Enlightened by such a realisation on the road to Hampstead, Fred stopped in his tracks, punched the summer air, and ran all the way back to Kilburn in search of Jack.

Much to his annoyance, the number of people lining the sides of the high road had quadrupled, at the very least, since he had set off for Hampstead. Newspapers that were only a few hours old crackled underfoot, discarded by a thronging mass with an insatiable thirst for fresh information. Anxiously, Fred wormed his way through the crowd, pushing and cursing as he did so. Ironically, it was Jack who found *him*. He had been trying in vain to get hold of a newspaper, and was on his way back to the shop. Unable to believe his luck, Fred stretched out his arms and drew Jack towards him. He had never been so happy to set eyes on someone in his life.

"Jacko!"

"Wha's go' into yer? An' why ain' yer at work?"

"Kitch'ner's beggin' for volun'eers, thousan's of 'em. Le's join up. You an' me."

"Join up!"

"Why no'? Oi, stop shovin'!" shouted Fred at the jostling profusion of elbows and knees around them. "It's a paid 'oliday abroad, Jacko. We'll never ge' another chance like it as long as we live!"

"Bu' wha' abou' Sis an' Frankie... I can' jus'..."

"Don' worry abou' *them*. They'll be all righ'. Res' of yer family'll take care of 'em... Cummon, Jacko! le' bygones be bygones, eh? Bofe of us need t'get away from 'ere an' all the memories."

"I dunno, Fred..."

"Course yer do. Cummon, there's no time t'waste. Guvmen's already called up all the reservists."

Around them, heads were turning, looking up from soiled newspapers, and Jack was painfully aware that his reply was awaited with bated breath by a group of strangers who had suddenly lost all interest in the printed war. Was it this oppressive air of expectancy that made him answer "I'll jus' le' Sis an' Ernest know firs'," or was it the prospect of getting away from a home and an entire area that reminded him constantly of Rose? Whatever his motive, it was a decision that he would later reflect on with very mixed, powerful feelings.

"'Ow'd they take it?" asked Fred, who had thought it best not to accompany Jack to the shop.

"Sis more or less guessed. She was a bi' upse', I think."

"She'll ge' over it. Tha' sis of yours 'as go' more pluck than the 'ole of the BEF pu' together. Any'ow, I've been askin' aroun', an' it looks like the bes' place t'enlis' is Poun' Lane."

Hours later, they were members of His Majesty's Armed Forces. They benefited immediately from this honour, because for the first time in their lives, courtesy of their new uniforms, they experienced the incomparable thrill of a gratuitous ride on public transport.

"If by chance you should discover one day in a restaurant that you are being served by a German waiter, you will throw the soup in his foul face; if you find yourself sitting at the side of a German clerk, you will spill the inkpot over his vile head."

"Does it really say that?"

"Yes...I must say, this Bottomley chap doesn't mince his words, does he? Course, he's only saying what the rest of us are thinking."

"There's no excuse for vulgarity," retorts Elisabeth, who finds such sentiments poetically unjustifiable and totally out of keeping with the noble aims of the Great Crusade Against Evil.

"Well if it wasn't for these Germans and Austrians we wouldn't be at war. They're the ones who're to blame."

"Blame or no blame, I still think it's wrong to talk about them in that way."

"All I know is we were doing very nicely before this war broke out. At this rate I'll be forced to close down. And what then?"

Elisabeth, who is in the process of clearing the table after supper, stops what she is doing and gazes down at her swinging gibbet. "Ernest," taking it in both hands, "it's high time I did the odd bit of domestic work again."

"You'll do no such thing! No wife of mine is going to..."

"Don't be so silly. We can't live on false pride."

"But what about Frankie? You can't take him with you, and you can't leave him here..."

"Lady's agreed to look after him."

"But she's already taking care of Louisa's children so *she* can..."

"I know, but now, through no fault of my own, I'm in the same predicament that she was, and Lady understands that. The family has to pull together, Ernest."

Mr Laurence thumps the copy of *John Bull*. "Blasted Kaiser! It's all *his* fault."

The Marshalls of Kensal Rise were fine, upstanding members of the community. Mr Marshall specialised in the modern art of painless dentistry, dutifully extracting, bridging and filling from nine in the morning to seven in the evening, six days a week. His good wife, who was a prominent figure in the British Women's Temperance Association, had been born with the enviable gift of dance. A generous woman, she imparted her god-given talent to those less gifted at the reasonable rate of a shilling an hour. Bearing in mind that the two of them worked at home, and that they had been blessed with four boys, it was fortunate they resided in a large, three-storey house. The ground floor was given over almost entirely to the surgery, a workshop, and a modest waiting room. Mrs Marshall's dance classes were held on the next floor up, in a spacious room that doubled as a splendid music room in rare moments of family leisure.

Their links with the Kitcheners were forged by an extremely young and surprisingly well-spoken Elisabeth, who, in 1909, became an integral part of the household in her capacity as a general domestic. Herbert and Irene Marshall, quick to recognise her natural grace and intelligence, urged Elisabeth to fulfil her potential by attending the College for Working Women. They even purchased a fine collection of books for her. It was therefore a bitter blow to them when she was forced by tragic circumstances to abandon her studies. Other domestics came and went in rapid succession until the welcome arrival of Mary.

Although by no means able to match her sister's refined qualities, she nevertheless possessed the unmistakable Kitchener devotion to duty. Moreover, she had a winsome personality that they found very endearing, particularly the boys. Owing to the additional presence of Mrs Marshall's bereaved and much-distressed sister, Mary was asked to continue living at home until adequate accommodation could be made available. Then, heralding the patter of millions of marching feet across the continent, the Great Foetus was born, and the accommodation problem duly solved. John Marshall, the couple's eldest son, was among the very first to answer his nation's desperate call to the colours, and in so doing, he left a billet door open in Kensal Rise for a love-sick general.

Violence breeds violence, they say. No one in their right mind would argue with this, of course, because no one in their right mind argues with a truism. What else could violence breed? Is it not a universal feature of the reproductive process that like yields like? Can a horse give birth to a tarantula, or vice-versa? Of course violence breeds violence. And as men from both sides ripped open a 140-mile stretch of Flanders soil that would safe-guard their lives as well as reclaim them (ashes to ashes); as the Allied grand masters pitted their combined wits against Schlief-fen's plan of attack, violence and its half-brother rivalry were also beginning to germinate away from the front. There was the violence inflicted on shop-fronts belonging to bakers, jewellers or hairdressers with names like Frieberger, Astrinsky, Sasse... Incensed crowds with an uncontrollable sense of duty to the realm went about their business undeterred by the small police presence, and even less by the odd poster that read, "I'm Russian. I'm one of the Allies". There was the violent abuse aim-ed at khakiless shirkers and their families, a form of abuse that would, in later years, be aimed with equal vehemence at the well-to-do who unpatriotically flaunted their well-to-do-ness in public. Last, but not least, and proving that some things never change, there was the continued violence waged against a defenceless army of pedestrians who *still* hadn't mastered the simple art of getting on and off buses safely, despite the many illustrations issued by the London General Omnibus Co. Ltd.

In the heady days of August 1914, when local parks were transformed into centres for hundreds of schoolless children and drilling volunteers, there was the honourable rivalry aroused by military parades. The dwellers of Kilburn, for instance, could justifiably boast that more troops marched through their high road (bound for St Albans via Edgware Road) than marched through the streets of Kensal Rise. Not to be outdone, the flag-bearing Kensalians gave vent to their patriotism by congregating on railway bridges frequented by troop trains. There was the honourable rivalry of recruitment, in which proud fathers with or without Boer War experience made a point of telling anyone who cared to listen that no less than three, four, five, six of his sons were serving King and Country. With the advent of conscription, this type of rivalry became redundant, so the emphasis shifted to the number and calibre of medals obtained by the fighting sons in question. There was the honourable rivalry of bereavement, arising, no doubt, from a need to come to terms with the tragic loss or losses. Consequently, "he died in the course of duty" was worth as much in the rivalry stakes as a V.C. (if not more). And there was the honourable rivalry prompted by officially-proclaimed questions such as "Are YOU doing all you can?" and "Daddy, what did YOU do in the Great War?" that would eventually lead to even middle-aged, flat-footed, hunch-backed sweet-shop owners being sworn in as 'special constables'.

The newspaper being pored over by Mr Laurence contains four or five crosses pencilled in at irregular intervals down the length of the domestic vacancies column. But his eyes are more interested in another column, which is headed, in clarendon type, *The War*.

"Here it is," he informs his two uniformed guests, clearing his throat. "'A Cricklewood man has returned from the trenches paralysed from rheumatism after spending a total of seventeen hours in trenches half-filled with water. The man, who is receiving treatment at Woolwich Hospital, spoke of the carnage he had witnessed, and claimed that many men were going mad.' There, I didn't want to alarm you, but, well, I just thought you ought to know."

"Fing is, me an' Jacko'll 'ave nothin' to do with trenches."

"How can you be so sure, Fred?" asks Elisabeth, who has spared no expense on the evening meal.

"Cos we'll be assigned ter the Royal 'Orse Artillery, tha's why. We'll be be'ind the lines takin' care of the 'orses."

"But Jack, you don't know the first thing about horses."

"Tha's jus' wha' I tol' Fred, Sis."

"Nuffink to it. Impor'an' fing t'remember bou' 'orses is tha' you treat 'em with respect. Tha' way they'll respec' yer back. Our bigges' problem'll be tryin' t'keep 'em calm when all them guns are goin' off, an' the bes' way t'do tha' is t'keep talkin' to 'em, nice an' soft, like yer would to yer sweet'eart."

"D'you think it will all be over by Christmas, like some people are saying?"

"Be surpised if it ain'. Tha's why I wonna ge' ou' there quick."

"We'll brin' yer a German 'elmet for Christmas," says Jack, eager to cheer up his sister.

The item read out by Mr Laurence had come as no surprise to Jack, and he could not help resenting his ex-employer for fanning Elisabeth's fears. Reports of that kind were rife during their daily training sessions. Furthermore, he did not share Fred's optimistic views concerning their non-involvement in trench warfare. If their job was simply to look after horses, why were they required to practise digging trenches lying face downwards, supposedly under fire? It was true that on hearing that Fred had worked as a carman, the two of them were sent out by Sergeant-Major Dulcken to commandeer as many horses as they could for the regiment, but this in no way made them automatic candidates for the RHA.

Putting a bold face on it, Elisabeth whisked the paper from under her husband's nose with the feigned gravity of a school mistress, and sighed, "That's enough war-talk for one day, I think." Then turning to Jack, she added, trying to keep the emotion out of her voice, "I can think of no better Christmas present this year than the safe return of all my brothers."

"Oi!" protested Fred. "Wha' abou' me?"

Boys will be boys, they say – *another* truism. What else could boys possibly be? Centipedes? Sticks of liquorice? But such considerations were the last thing on Mary's mind as she cheered and jumped up and down on a sunlit afternoon in late August together with hundreds of other tumultuous patriots. The three Marshalls huddled around her were also cheering and jumping up and down. Arnold, Matthew and George, aged eight, seven and six respectively, were obviously too young to accompany their brother John to the Western Front, yet even little boys will be boys. Mary, who had discreetly pretended not to notice (just as she had earlier pretended to herself that she was not being followed), put it down precisely to that, and to the fact that they were extremely thrilled by the occasion. Each time the lookouts shouted "'Ere comes anuvver one!", a huge roar greeted the news. And as it steamed closer and closer, the volume of the singing increased proportionately, until the sound of hundreds of voices intoning 'Rule Britannia' reached a clamorous climax that coincided perfectly with the point at which the approaching train thundered past, rocking the very foundations of the bridge and engulfing all the assembled in billows of steam. At breathtaking moments such as these, it was only natural that the Marshall boys, who, through no fault of their own, were pressed tightly against their young nanny, should allow their hands and cheeks to touch anatomical areas that, under normal circumstances, they would have respectfully steered well clear of. This innocent expression of boyish excitement was admirably tolerated by a domestic who was plainly years ahead of her time. In fact, so anxious was she to play the whole thing down, that instead of pulling away at the critical moments, she chose those very same moments, when song, train and steam were one, to place her arms around little Arnold, Matthew and George in a warm, sisterly embrace, hold her breath, and thrill to the excitement of it all.

The unparalleled mass-worshipping of Britain's most celebrated lady notwithstanding, it was not Britannia who ruled, but Dora, that equally celebrated custodian of the nation's welfare. Following her meteoric rise to fame, Dora, the new personification of Britain, wasted no time at all in preparing for the arrival of the deadly storks commonly known as "gasbags". Dora doused London's lighting by curtaining buses and trams; turning off car headlights; smearing street lamps with blue paint, and blinding the windows of houses. And while the entire metropolis slept under this mantle of darkness, the tireless Defender (an obvious forerunner of the Super Hero and Heroine) probed the night skies with spotlights of gargantuan proportions worthy of her own incredible powers.

What a comfort it was to know that these powers extended to defending Britons from themselves, since what good was it trying to ward off the Godless Hun if endemic evils were left unattended? And could any Sassenach in the whole of Albion, Bible in hand, deny that by far and away the greatest evil in the land was the self-destructive abuse of alcohol? Knowing that the name of the game was asceticism; that the Show could not run for long without it, public houses were therefore obliged to stop being public after 11 pm. For the public's further Dorian protection and benefit, this was later brought forward to 10 pm.

Mrs Marshall, of course, was among the first to applaud the act.

No performer can ever do justice to a part without thoroughly rehearsing it first. Lines, cues, entrances, and a host of other important details must be grasped. Only then, word-perfect and immersed in the intricacies of the role, can he or she take to the boards with confidence. The untried cast of the Command Performance was no different in this respect. Up and down the same national decks where not so long ago deserting rats had scampered, could now be heard the heart-warming sound of khakied and Kitchener-blued men alike getting to grips with the heroic characters that King and Country expected them to represent. Under the expert coaching of company officers, they quickly learnt how to shoot and bayonet with deadly accuracy, and how to load a Japanese Arisaka-type rifle literally with their eyes shut (on the actual night they would use the standard service rifle: the short-magazine Lee-Enfield); they learnt how to dig trenches with entrenching tools, and how to disguise them with sods and gorse bushes or other shrubs; they learnt how to crawl through prickles and mud, and, above all, they learnt how to grin and bear the eternal marching.

Rehearsals usually got underway with 5 am reveille, after which, from 6:15 to 7:15, a strenuous physical drill would be held. Following a short breakfast around 8, the whole battalion then marched to its allotted area for more fatigues. They were normally back at base by 2 pm, leaving the enlisted thespians free for the day.

It was at precisely that stage in the proceedings, on a blustery afternoon early in September, that Sergeant-Major Dulcken instructed the men to fall in. All the signs were that the great curtain-call had finally arrived. It could be felt in the air as Major H.J. Alderman tilted his head back, and commenced his address.

"Men, as I've no need to remind any of you, there's no greater honour than to be asked to serve one's country. Well, that honour, I'm proud to tell you, has just been bestowed on this battalion." Cheering soldiers congratulate one another under the reproving eye of their sergeant-major. "Yes, men, at long last, we've got our marching orders!" More jubilation and unprofessional breaking of ranks. "To those of you who didn't hesitate to join us, who only last month were working as bank clerks, and labourers, and what have you, I have this to say: no doubt those who enlist after you will enjoy the luxury of more prolonged training. Who knows? they might even miss out on active service altogether. Well, I can honestly say to you that at least in *my* opinion, you're as ready as you'll ever be! I can say, without the slightest hesitation, that you can and jolly well *will* do us proud."

Amid the celebrations, a certain Private Kitchener exchanges an unmistakable look with a certain Private Russell. It reads: "So much for us being assigned to the RHA."

As far as everybody present was concerned, it was only a Last Supper in the sense that it was a prelude to an inevitable farewell. That was where the similarity with the famous repast ended. Yes, there were certainly tears in eyes and a veritable colony of frogs in throats, and an out-of-the-ordinary emphasis placed on nostalgic recollections, but there was no underlying awareness of impending sacrifice. In the eyes of youngsters like Peter and

James, it was honourable envy rather than resigned grief which sparkled like the golden light on the buttons of their older brothers' tunics. The same envy could also be seen smouldering in the oldest pair of eyes at the head of the table.

As fate would have it, the five Kitchener boys had received their mobilisation orders within days of each other, despite the fact that only George and Hubert had joined the same regiment. Was it thus any wonder that a humble feast was laid on to mark the occasion, and that all the Kitcheners and all the wedded partners and all the children (and Fred) were there to partake of it? No, not even Mary was absent on that most memorable of nights. To the welcome surprise of the family, a remarkable transformation had occurred. Gone were the monosyllabic mumbles; gone were her scathing looks of resentment, and gone too was the disturbing air of reckless abandon that had descended on her after the disappearance of Billy. The change was almost too... It was so remarkable that... There was something not quite... Surely the young man hadn't...

But now Elisabeth is rising with solemn poise, clutching not a cross (there is no awareness of impending sacrifice) but one of her beloved books of poetry. Very slowly, the silence she requires replaces the warm din of excitement.

"I'd like to read some lines from a poem by Keats. Although it's called 'To My Brother George', rest assured that it's meant for all of you." She looks towards the assembled uniforms. "'I see the lark down-dropping to his nest, / And the broad winged sea gull never at rest; / For when no more he spreads his feathers free, / His breast is dancing on the restless sea. / Now I direct my eyes into the west, / Which at this moment is in sunbeams dressed: / Why westward turn? 'Twas but to say adieu! / 'Twas but to kiss my hand, dear George, to you!'"

She blows her brothers a kiss, and, rather bashfully, they smile and clap their hands. There is more clapping when Frank rises to his feet with the evident intention of saying a few words. "Sons, do wha' you've gotta do, an' for 'eavens sake do it well. Ender speech!"

The brevity of his contribution prompts a rapturous round of applause, much laughter, and the raising of glasses. Edward, who is now full of respect for the supernatural powers-that-be which he once cursed, has something to tell the family. Before doing so, however, he asks to be handed his two daughters. Alice is fast asleep on her grandmother's lap, and so is none the wiser when she is placed over her father's shoulder. In sharp contrast, Lottie is a wriggling bundle of energy who giggles with delight when perched on his other arm. On seeing this, Frankie rushes to Jack's side and demands to be sat on his knee.

"Mum, Dad...an' ev'ryone, 'specially the lit'le uns," Edward plants a kiss on his children's cheeks, "none of us are gonna le'cher down. The Boche is gonna ge' wha' it deserves, 'ave no doub' abou' tha'. I'm jus' grateful this war came now, when I can do somink abou' it. I'm goin' ou' there t'get as many of 'em as I can." Cheers from Peter and James. "*All* of us are. An' when we ge' back, we're gonna see oo's been the deadlies' sho'. Ooever comes back wivver longes' lis' ge's trea'ed by all the others to a nigh' onner town – *wha'ever* the missus says!"

Laughter and clapping all round the table. In the intoxicating atmosphere, the old maxim that right is might is elevated to unquestioned heights of divine, infallible law – and the same is happening across the nation as a whole.

Play. A Drum and Fife band is on hand to escort the marching volunteers from the 9th Battalion Middlesex Territorial Regiment at Pound Lane via Harlesden to Willesden Junction Station. They are accompanied by hundreds of relatives along the way. Civilians are not allowed on the platforms, and so the hasty farewells take place outside the station. Inside, special trains bound for Sheerness let off impatient bursts of steam. Finally, the men having disentangled themselves from their tearful loved ones, the trains pull slowly out. At Sheerness, large crowds wave farewell to embarking troops. Destination: France.

"Goodbye, Jack!" shouts Elisabeth, hoisting his son high above her head.

Six

Treaties, as Lloyd George coined it, are the currency of international statesmanship. Scraps of paper or not, they are diplomatic legal tender, and should therefore be honoured at all costs. I promise to pay the bearer... But what if the administrative coffers are, uhum! a little on the thin side?

Yes, indeed, the name of this all-embracing, ascetic game was 'Cut It Out'. The rules were simple enough: never, ever cheat (or contemplate cheating), and if you can go without, and even if you cannot, *do*. An interesting part of the game consisted in seeing how much tighter an already tight belt could be tightened. If you could still breathe and were not suffering from dizzy spells, you knew that you were almost certainly not being as hard on yourself as you should. This constituted an infringement of the rules as well as letting down the side.

Another part of the game involved training the mind never to lose sight of the fact that unnecessary greed at home equalled a hungry, treaty-defending soldier in Flanders. This was probably the easiest part to play because, generally, it is the flesh that is weak, not the mind. So as bread and butter became increasingly harder to get hold of, and gas prices rose from 2/6 to 2/8, and rates soared by 4d in the pound, and bus routes were seriously disrupted owing to the war demand on the fleet, the precious equation 'civilian greed = military shortage' was borne scrupu-lously in mind by the vast majority of players.

Winner? What winner? Abstemious participation, like virtue, was its own, inestimable reward.

"Mary."

"Yes, Mrs Marshall?"

"I heard it *again*, last night."

"Heard wha'?"

"You know, that noise I told you about."

"Oh..."

"I'm afraid it's beginning to upset the boys. Are you *sure* you didn't find any traces of mice or rats up there?"

"I can 'ave another look, if yer like."

"Would you, dear? You're *such* a brave girl."

"I'll go up there righ' now."

"The boys *will* be pleased."

Mary removes her apron and, followed by an *ever so grateful* Mrs Marshall, makes her way to the top of the house. The young domestic has been decidedly off-colour these past few weeks. Surprisingly, no one has noticed that her eyes are swollen and ringed, or the unusually high number of times that she yawns in the course of a day. Perhaps they *have* noticed, but simply put it down to her workload, or even, of course – yes, that would explain it – to the nights that she surely lies awake thinking of her poor brothers.

Mr Marshall, it must be said, does not share his wife's unrest. Exhausted after a long, hard day of hunched toil in the endless battle against caries, he sleeps like the proverbial log from the moment his head touches the pillow. A man committed to the belief that hard work is morally edifying, he attributes his wife's recent obsession with things that apparently go bump in the night to the fact that circumstances beyond their control have forced her to suspend her dance classes. (A woman committed to the belief that man does not live by bread alone, Mrs Marshall refuses to teach shirkers, and since those who are not shirkers are either busy preparing for war in drill halls, or are already on active service abroad; and since the sweethearts they have left behind have no partners with which to waltz or polka, the pool of her existing and potential clients has dramatically but, hopefully, only temporarily, dried up.) It has also crossed the industrious dentist's mind that the influence exerted on his wife by her sister Victoria being anything but salutary, the strange obsession with nocturnal raps might well have something to do with her. (A woman committed to the belief that if the Almighty had intended us to be happy, He would not have created *un*happiness, she is a natural devotee of gloom, so what with losing a husband; war being declared, and London blacked out, her faith has never been stronger.)

"Victoria, dear," calls Mrs Marshall when they have reached the uppermost landing. A partially-opened door reveals an indistinct form curled up on the bed. "She's resting," Mary is informed with lowered voice. "It's been *such* a trying time for her. Now then, is the ladder in place? Good. And you've got your candle... *Do* be careful, dear."

"I'll be all righ'," says Mary, her enlarged silhouette trembling on the loft entrance.

She raises the trap-door, positions the candlestick inside, and, with a ruffle of petticoats, climbs gracefully into the loft.

No period-piece would ever be complete without its fair share of costumes. The 1914 production of *The Great War* was no exception. Despite the centuries' old, West End success of *The Monarchy*, with its castles and palaces, and its truly incomparable pomp and ceremony, the relatively unspectacular array associated with the armed forces nevertheless succeeded in winning over the British public. In the opening scenes, for instance, the mere sight of khaki or Kitchener blue was enough to precipitate a standing ovation of unparalleled fervour. The sound of army boots on cobble-stone; the beat of a parading drum, were enough to set the pulse a-racing. The operatic virtuosity of a sergeant-major's bellowed commands was enough to leave a sizeable lump in the throat. Towards the end of the First Act, however, a new uniform appeared on the scene. Prompted, no doubt, by the bright blue, red and white that distinguished it, the audience's initial reaction was one of hilarity – here come the clowns! Every great work requires its emotional respites, and these loudly-hued buffoons were just the characters to provide them. Imagine, therefore, the widespread sense of disquiet when it became clear that the hobbling men clad in Union Jacks were not clowns at all, but wounded soldiers brought home from the front. Realising its mistake, the audience leapt to its feet, and was about to unite in a round of deafening applause when, quite unexpectedly, a special constable walked on stage. He was dragging a bale of hay, and holding up a banner which read: 'Quiet for the wounded.' Respectfully, everybody sat down again, whereupon the SC began scattering straw outside all the military hospitals.

Unlike her own cross, the four or five that Elisabeth had pencilled in at irregular intervals down the length of the domestic vacancies column brought her no comfort whatsoever. Such was the financial burden imposed on lower, middle and upper working class housewives by the continuing male exodus, that for every local vacancy, there were at least a dozen or so applicants (the idea of war-work for women of this ilk had yet to get off the ground). Despite her previous experience and her impressive references, Elisabeth was unable to find an opening locally, and was thus forced to try her luck further afield – Hampstead, to be precise. In so doing, she would complete a circle of coincidence initiated almost three and a half years earlier in High Road Kilburn under a red, muted lion.

It is the first week of October, and a fierce wind sweeps through Fitzjohn's Avenue. Elisabeth is almost blown over, and has to hold on with Pankhurstian determination to an iron railing. While thus secured, a volley of dead leaves catches her by surprise, inflicting a slight flesh wound. When she eventually reaches 1 Prince Arthur Road, a tear of blood divides her right cheek. Seemingly unmoved by this, an elderly butler with an all-too-familiar stoop leads her silently into a spacious study.

There are books everywhere! From corner to corner, floor to ceiling, there are shelves upon shelves of them. Elisabeth has never seen a collection like it. Perusing one gilded title after another, she runs an enraptured finger over their soft, leather-bound spines. She would do anything to own a room like this! Imagine it: sinking into that fine armchair over there with a volume in your hands and not a single demand on your time, surrounded by the consecrated likes of...

"Mrs Laurence?"

She gasps, and instinctively clutches her cross as she turns round.

"Oh, I startled you. Do forgive me – but your cheek, it's bleeding."

Elisabeth touches her face and feels a thread of dried blood.

"I'll ask Burchfield to bring a little water. I shan't be a minute."

"Thank you, but there's really no..."

"It's the least we can do. Please sit down."

Although feeling a little dazed, the general domestic still has sufficient wits about her to eschew the splendid armchair and select a lesser piece more in keeping with her station. Being jolted out of a fanciful daydream in unfamiliar surroundings and then being treated to such kindness has rather disconcerted her.

"Here, you can wipe your face with this – there's a flannel inside."

Elisabeth reaches for the small china bowl, but it is not handed over to her. "Oh, I might as well do it – no point both of us getting our hands wet."

"Oh no, I've put you to enough trouble as it is."

"Nonsense, it's no trouble at all. Now keep still a moment."

The softness of the flannel on her skin and the delicate care with which it is applied help soothe Elisabeth's nervous unease.

"I think a leaf grazed my cheek on my way here."

"I'm not surprised with this awful gale. There we are...as good as new."

"Thank you ever so much."

"Don't mention it."

Elisabeth prepares herself for the formal commencement of the interview, but the interviewer's friendly smile is followed by silence, not questions. It is a relaxed, uncontrived silence which invites genuine conversation as opposed to nervous chatter.

"When you came in," begins Elisabeth in response to the tacit invitation, "I was so busy admiring your wonderful collection that I quite forgot the purpose of my visit."

"I can see you adore books as much as I do. I spend hours in here every day."

"How I envy you," remarks Elisabeth, good-naturedly.

"Oh, you mustn't envy me – you see, I can picture you in the very-near future sitting in that delightful armchair over there, reading to your heart's content."

Struck dumb by this, Elisabeth can only gape in astonishment at her prospective employer.

"You *will* accept the post, won't you?"

"Yes – yes of course I will, but..."

"That's settled then. When can you start?"

"Right away."

"Good."

Miss Dill smiles in the knowledge that she and the pleasantly-bemused Mrs Laurence are going to get on very well indeed.

Affinity, affinity, a kingdom for affinity. Not all domestics were as fortunate in this respect as Elisabeth, whose working relationship with Miss Dill blossomed into a caring friendship in no time at all. Of course, no servant ever expects to be befriended by those that he or she serves, but a modicum of decency *is* expected. Louisa, who had originally counted herself lucky to find employment so quickly, subsequently rued the day that a Mr and Mrs Fowler took her on.

To begin with, though, the childless Fowlers had seemed the perfect employers. They were kind and reasonable, and had proved this by readily agreeing that Louisa was needed at home by her two daughters, and would therefore not be a resident domestic. Staunch patriots, they spoke in glorious terms of the great sacrifice being made by the humble men and women of Britain in the defence of freedom. Questions concerning the whereabouts and welfare of Edward were for ever on their lips. Then, inevitably, it happened. Why inevitably? Well, certain factors have to be taken into consideration, and assumptions made. Some women are blessed (or perhaps cursed) with an inherent sexual allure which they can intensify, if they so wish, but not suppress. It may be compared to a sensual frequency which they are constantly transmitting – with or without a specific receiver in mind; wittingly or unwittingly. From what we can piece together, it is fairly safe to assume that Louisa was such a woman. This has to be borne in mind when analysing the uncivil behaviour of the Fowlers. Mrs Fowler, it is equally safe to assume, did not possess, and hence did not exude, this particular quality. Aged fifty-four, the passing years had, to put it rather bluntly, fallen upon her like the butcher's axe falls on a carcass: she was desperately lean, her face, like her body, a fearsome symmetry of shadows trapped in bony hollows. Yet despite her emaciated appearance, she somehow managed to consume twice as much food as her husband. The likeliest explanation is that she was beset with tumours, although existing medical records make no mention of this. Turning to Mr Fowler, it is also equally safe to assume that the former alderman and successful merchant received Louisa's signal 'loud and clear'. Starved, in all probability, of his libidinous needs through no fault of his own, or, for that matter, of his cadaverous wife (she had discharged her final menses almost a decade earlier), is it any wonder that what happened, happened?

The strength of the induced lure can be gauged by Mr Fowler's unpatriotic breaking of the 'Cut It Out' rules. Totally out of character, and proving that the flesh *is* weaker than the mind, he actually contemplated cheating, and felt quite unable to go without. And far from tightening his belt for the good of the nation, he became completely obsessed with thoughts of undoing it altogether...

"Ah, there you are," he says, entering the kitchen. Louisa greets him with a cordial smile, and continues unloading two large baskets laden with provisions. "You were gone, er, quite some time. Long queues, I expect..."

"They ge' longer every day, an' tryin' t'ge' 'old of but'er nowadays..."

"It's to be expected with a war on... Any news of Edward?"

Louisa shakes her head. "Still, no news is good news."

"Yes...I, er, expect you're missing him a great deal."

"Yeah, bu' there's loadsa women in the same boa' as me. You jus' pu' up with it and ge' on with things."

"But...you must get very lonely sometimes."

"I try not ter think abou' it too much, to be hones'."

"No, quite. Oh, by the way, Louisa, Mrs Fowler wasn't feeling herself this morning, so, um, I suggested she lie down for a few hours – you know, put her feet up."

"Is there anythin' I can do for 'er?"

"No, she just needs plenty of rest, that's all. I dare say you must be a bit tired yourself after carrying all that lot. Tell you what: sit down and I'll make you a nice cup of tea."

"Oh there's really no need for tha', Mr..."

"You're too strong for your own good, Louisa, that's your trouble."

This time, appreciative of her master's exemplary concern, her smile is a heartfelt one.

"It's kind of yer t'offer, bu'..."

"I won't take no for an answer," he insists jovially, antennae twitching as they pick up the unmistakable frequency emitted by her smile. "So you sit yourself down, and I'll put the kettle on." Still smiling, she pulls out a chair from under the kitchen table and sits down. "Here, you can put your feet up on this."

Her smile broadens still further as he places an old crate by her feet. "I really don' know wha' I've done t'deserve this."

"All work and no play – you know what they say, Louisa."

He strides across the room with a youthful spring in his step. A kettle rests on the gas cooker. However, after several unsuccessful attempts to light it, Louisa feels obliged to show him how it should be done. "You've gotta ge' the end of the taper in jus' the righ' place or it won' ligh'," she informs him, lighting the burner at the first time of trying. "See? There's nothin' to it!"

But poor, unsuspecting Louisa! Poor besotted Mr Fowler! She had kindled a great deal more than a flame. As she reached across the stove, the glimpse of curly, matted hair under her arm; the pronounced profile of her breast; the suggestive tightening of fabric over her hips and rump – it was all too much for him. Sexual feelers ablur with misconstrued messages; as much a victim of his blinding misconceptions as she of her irrepressible signals, the former civic dignitary, his self-control overcome by the fumes of a raging passion, locked his arms around the object of his desire, pressed mouth against mouth, and groin against groin. Louisa, who had not yet parted company with the smouldering taper, struggled free of his clutches and uttered a breathless, "Mr Fowler!" His anguished retort left her stunned: "For God's sake have some pity, woman!" And no doubt convinced that actions would shed more light on his meaning than words, his frenzied eyes fixed intimidatingly on hers, he undid his belt-buckle, his trouser-buttons, and bared his painfully erect self to Louisa. Curiously, however, the anger, revulsion and shock that she genuinely felt did not prevent her from experiencing another response: from one of those mysterious recesses of the mind, a distant voice sounding remarkably like her own could be heard evaluating the merits and general characteristics of the throbbing member with extraordinary dispassion. Its length and width, together with its barrel-like solidity, were deemed in excess, and well in excess, of any that she had ever encountered. Who knows precisely where these clinical, if involuntary, deliberations would have led if the voice had not been drowned by the horrific shriek simultaneously elicited from her lips by the red-hot taper in her hand and by the thick, creamy gell that suddenly, inevitably, spurted towards her? But drowned it most certainly was, and the answer to this question, though seemingly obvious, is destined to remain a matter of conjecture.

The rest, all too predictably, acquired a rather pathetic air. Guilt-mumbled apologies; hasty pulling up of garments; aggrieved mopping of yellowish slime from dress... And although Mr Fowler vowed never again to fall 'fowl' of the 'Cut It Out' rules, or of any others (a vow he succeeded in honouring), master-servant relations deteriorated from that incident onwards. The main cause of this was not Mr but *Mrs* Fowler, for she had been quick to notice that whenever her husband and Louisa happened to be in the same room, a dark current of emotions flowed between them – and dark currents could only mean one thing: they shared a dark secret. When she confronted her husband with her suspicions, he flatly denied that they were having an affair. Mrs Fowler was duly persuaded by his heartfelt denial; but terrified that his wife was not as convinced as she claimed, that she might consider securing total peace of mind by dismissing Louisa (providing her with a golden opportunity to reveal the sordid truth), Mr Fowler decided to allay any lingering doubts his wife might have by treating the domestic with marked contempt whenever possible. The luckless Louisa was privately informed that this was the only way he could guarantee she held onto her job. But his callous behaviour towards her could not conceal the fact, in Mrs Fowler's mind, that there was definitely "something going on" between them. Applying some rudimentary logic to the situation, she surmised that her husband's innocence presupposed Louisa's guilt. Yes, the woman was clearly a common harlot, a ruthless Jezebel plotting to entice Mr Fowler away from her as a replacement for the cuckold on the front whose days were surely numbered. As she became increasingly convinced of this treacherous scenario, and her conduct towards Louisa changed accordingly, the innocent victim became increasingly and conversely convinced that Mrs Fowler was a cruel and nasty sack of bones who was jealous of her good looks and the possible effects these might have on her husband.

Not surprisingly, she considered leaving and finding employment elsewhere, but times, as everyone kept saying, were hard and getting even harder. So Louisa gritted her teeth, and gradually she developed a duck-like resistance to the waves of abuse that rolled her way if, perchance, she arrived for work a minute late, or if the tiniest speck of dust came to Mrs Fowler's critical attention.

The first snow of winter floats to the ground with icy insouciance. Its haphazard descent is watched by Mr Laurence from the relative warmth of his deserted shop. Stooped over his counter, the picturesque scene outside reminds him that it will soon be Christmas, usually the most profitable time of the year. He glances down dejectedly at the piece of cardboard in his hands: *Closed until further notice.* Frosty half-moons have already encrusted themselves on the window panes when, with a resigned shake of the head, he secures the sign to the door and pulls down the blind. The stupid farce is over. Millions of able-bodied earners are otherwise engaged; taxation has risen to crippling levels... Who in their right mind is going to squander what little money they have on the transient luxuries contained in a bag of pear drops or sherbets? He shall just have to follow Elisabeth's advice and swallow his false sense of pride. If he has to depend on her, then so be it. Necessity is also the mother of compromise. No use delving into his meagre savings quite yet.

However...there is no escaping that ubiquitous finger and its insatiable appetite for civilians (didn't anyone ever tell him it was rude to point!) According to his local paper, the finger has recently developed a liking for fit men over forty-five. Well, fit he most certainly is not. But the beckoning digit is not so easily eluded, for not a day goes by without news reaching his ears that old So-and-so has decided to become a special constable. The insurmountable problem here is simply that age, unfitness and physical deformities are no obstacle: with an awareness of the concept of equal opportunities that is decades ahead of its time, everyone and anyone is allowed to be an unpaid, uniformed accessory to the overworked police force. The country expects *each* man to do his duty. And however much pride you manage to swallow, there is always some in reserve. Consequently, if it boils down to a choice between incurring the belittling disdain of those around you (epitomised by the pinning of a white feather on your lapel by an irate young lady) and succumbing to the ubiquitous, insatiable, beckoning pressure in your midst, you elect the latter. There are no viable excuses when you suddenly find yourself with an awful lot of time on your hands. Blasted Kaiser!

1 Prince Arthur Road was more than just a house in Hampstead. To Elisabeth, it was a unique haven in a world of increasing hardship and austerity; it was a literary and spiritual retreat; a rich oasis for her beleagured emotions; a much-loved sanctuary from all that was threatening.

Since swallowing the bitter pill of his pride, Mr Laurence had himself been imbued with a bitterness that made relations between them more strained than usual. The parabolic obsequiousness that his trade had both fostered and provided a daily outlet for had now degenerated into an irritating fretfulness. The virtual break in sexual relations, for which Elisabeth alone was responsible, did little to alleviate the situation. They began to quarrel as never before, although, to their credit, Frankie was never exposed to it.

Contrary to what Elisabeth had hoped, Mr Laurence's querulous ways were not changed for the better by his joining the ranks of the Special Constabulary. The dark blue uniform that he had so reluctantly donned had introduced him to Power (the two did not recall ever having met). Suddenly, the fawning sweet-seller was a zealous enforcer of Dorian law (they took to each other immediately). Had it been physically possible, SC Laurence would have walked the streets with his head held high. However, he felt and therefore gave the distinct impression of being a good three or four inches taller.

Elisabeth, whose innate prescience had mysteriously flourished in the company of Miss Dill, knew full well where the abrupt transformation would lead. The childish bickering over meals or finance was just the beginning. It was only a matter of time.

But at least from morning to evening, life was pure bliss. Her domestic duties in the Dill household were minimal. In fact, she was called upon to act more as a nurse than a servant. Miss Dill's mother had been confined to her bed for the past fifteen years. Large and extremely overweight, the daily task of changing her linen and tending to her personal needs was all the more awkward. In the pre-war days, a private army of specially-trained attendants had made light work of it. Now, though, with the family business not as profitable as it might otherwise have been if Mrs Dill's three sons had not swapped their city suits for their country's colours (Mr Dill had died of a sudden heart attack in 1911), and with a desperate shortage of manpower, they were reduced to a token butler and a single domestic. Burchfield's age and ailing frame meant that the arduous nursing chores were shared by Elisabeth and Miss Dill, who was not the least bit perturbed by the 'unseemly' demands that circumstances were making of her.

When the two women were not attending to Mrs Dill, they were to be found either in the kitchen or, as was more often the case, in their revered study.

"I don't know about you," says Miss Dill, comically flexing her biceps, "but all this work with mamma is beginning to show. Here, feel!"

Amused by the suggestion, Elisabeth leans forward and lays her hand on the firm ball of muscle shrouded by a silken sleeve.

"You're meant to press it!" laughs Miss Dill, placing her own hand on Elisabeth's and pushing it down into her arm. "That's better!"

"It feels harder than a blacksmith's," remarks Elisabeth, her hand still sandwiched by Miss Dill's own hand and her arm.

"Well, having never laid a finger on a blacksmith in all my life, I'll just have to take your word for it."

"Oh, you ought to try it. You have no idea what you're missing!"

Elisabeth bursts out laughing, and although Miss Dill is also amused, her expression is but a veil over another one: serious, contemplative...

"I can't say I find *that* idea very appealing."

"Oh really? What *do* you find appealing, then?"

The expression is unveiled, and a long, unsmiling look passes between them. Slowly, almost imperceptibly, Miss Dill's fingers commence their artful caress. Elisabeth shuts her eyes, her own fingers coming tentatively to life upon the silken arm. Moments later, the study door opens, and they pull discreetly away.

"Ah, the tea," says Miss Dill, rising to meet the lanky figure of Burchfield.

After passing her a silver tray with shaking hands, he departs without uttering a word. When Miss Dill places the salver on the table with an exaggerated trembling of the arms, Elisabeth cannot help dissolving into laughter. "Poor Burchfield," sighs Miss Dill, pouring out the tea. "I sometimes wonder where the old boy summons the strength to breathe in and out."

Tears roll down Elisabeth's cheeks. "I haven't laughed like this in years."

"Come now," responds Miss Dill, wiping away Elisabeth's tears with her fingertips, "it isn't *that* funny."

"I suppose it's because I haven't had much to laugh about recently."

"The last time *I* laughed so much was just before poor papa died. We were singing songs around the piano, all of us, when, all of a sudden, there was an enormous bang. A gust of air had blown the door shut. It gave us such an awful fright that the notes froze in our throats. But what was so funny was that we still looked as if we were singing. You can imagine the kind of faces we were pulling!"

She purses her lips, bellies her cheeks, and crosses her eyes. Elisabeth sheds fresh tears before disclosing that she cannot even remember the last time she laughed so much.

"Oh, you're not getting out of it that easily. Come on, think back."

"I can't think of anything that made me..."

"But there must be something!"

"Well, there was the time when Jack took an old Holland-cover and pretended to be a ghost."

"You call *that* funny?"

"It was at the time!"

"How old were you?"

"About seven or eight."

"No wonder you found it funny, then... You poor thing," adds Miss Dill, squeezing Elisabeth's hand, "it *is* a long time since you had a really good laugh."

"Yes," comes the suddenly self-conscious reply.

Miss Dill smiles and wraps the fingers of both hands around her tea cup. "You know what *is* funny? – peculiar, not ha-ha. They're calling us the surplus women."

"The surplus women!"

"Yes, the poor women who can't find a man because they're all away fighting."

Elisabeth nods, averting her gaze.

"But come to think of it, you're not in the least bit surplus. You have Mr Laurence, don't you?"

"Yes, I do."

"It's the likes of *me* who are supposed to be surplus. Oh, I do so hate being lumped together like that. I mean, it's not as if we're all the same, is it?"

"No. Any news of your brothers yet?"

Miss Dill sighs and settles back in her chair. "No...it's been three months now. Mamma's putting a brave face on it, but she must be beside herself with worry – especially with Christmas being so close. We'd love to send them something, but no one will tell us where they are."

"Or us."

"And the winter we're having! I know the government's doing all it can collecting woollies to send over, but it isn't the same as sending it to them yourself, is it?"

"It must be hellish out there," says Elisabeth, feeling a sudden pang of guilt.

Was nothing even remotely sacred?

An understanding populace had witnessed and cheered the

mobilisation of its young men; the commandeering of its buses, trains and horses by His Majesty's loyal servants. It had patriotically accepted the early closing of its cherished public houses; tolerated the blackouts; the spiralling rate of taxation; the censoring of correspondence...but even those who had willingly toed the line for the greater good, whose belts seriously threatened to rend them asunder, even *they* must have been hard pressed not to harbour mutinous thoughts when the Cricklewood Skating Rink was appropriated by the government for use, of all things, as a workshop! Did not the local community owe the stability of its family life to this hallowed rink? (Communities here, there and everywhere were similarly affronted, for possession orders of this kind were sadly rife.) Was Dora not aware of the number of citizens whose hearts had permanently intertwined to the rousing music of eccentrically-named band leaders? What sort of a woman was she? How could she possibly fail to appreciate that certain buildings in the land were inviolable because clinging to every chandelier, adhered to every baluster, ingrained in every inch of polished floor was a loving, life-sustaining memory as immortal as the Elysian lily? Had not the fathers and mothers of those gallant Tommies been right to expect that their sentimental store-houses would be safe from institutionalised desecration?

Yet, to their eternal credit, convinced that their war effort was indeed a crusade against Evil that simply had to be won if decency and justice were to prevail, they accepted their fate with a steadfastness and a courage rivalled only by the boys (*their* boys) on the front.

"Name?"

"Ernest V. Laurence."

"What's the V for?"

"Victor."

"Age?"

"Fifty-two."

"Right, Mr Laurence, if you'd care to put your hand on this bible and repeat after me: 'I swear by Almighty God and His Majesty, King George V...'"

"'I swear by Almighty God and His Majesty, King George V...'"

"'...that I do willingly and without coercion...'"
"'...that I do willingly and without coercion...'"
"'...offer my services as a Special Constable...'"
"'...offer my services as a Special Constable...'"
"'...until such time as they are no longer required.'"
"'...until such time as they are no longer required.'"
"Right, Mr...Laurence, that gentleman over there will take care of you now. Next!"

Try as she might, Mary cannot stop her teeth chattering. The scullery is cold – as cold, or so it seems to her, as the frozen garden onto which it looks out. Not even the thought of her nocturnal ascent to paradise can abate the bony cacophony inside her head, less still the numbing pain inflicted on her fingers by the icy water. One evening, she lost all sensation in her feet, and resorted to jumping up and down on the spot. Slowly, enough heat was generated to melt the two blocks of ice. Encouraged by this, she adopted the habit of arching forward onto her toes and backwards onto her heels while washing the dishes (jumping on the spot was too strenuous and likely to precipitate the breaking of a glass or a piece of china). When, on one occasion, her callisthenics were noticed by Mr Marshall, he quipped, "Been taking lessons from Mrs Marshall, have we?" but he showed no concern whatsoever about the arctic conditions in which she was obliged to work.

The last dish is wiped clean. She dries her hands vigorously on an old towel, and walks towards the dining room, from where a warm glow radiates. "Beggin' yer pardon, will yer be needin' me any more tonigh'?" "Mary," says Mrs Marshall, who, like her husband, is seated before a roaring fire, "there's something we'd like to talk to you about, *isn't there*, dear?" "I suppose so," mumbles Mr Marshall. Mary tries not to look as alarmed as she feels while surrendering to the lure of the hearth. "That's right, dear, warm yourself up. It gets colder by the day, doesn't it? Poor Victoria, she never could cope with winter. That's why she spends most of her time in bed these days." "It's called hibernation," says Mr Marshall. "Tortoises do it." "It's nothing of the sort, Herbert... Now, Mary, it's about those noises in the loft. We've *all* heard them now." "Can' imagine wha's causin' it." "Well, it's

quite obviously a rodent of some kind. What else could it be?"
"Don' know." "Mr Marshall and I agree that the filthy beasts
must be hiding in the straw. Whatever possessed him to cover
the attic floor with layers of straw is something I'll *never* know."
"To trap the heat! How many times do I have to tell you it's called
insula..." "Never mind what it's called. If you ask me, that chappie who talked you into it was talking a load of nonsense." "He's
a builder, Irene! He's done the same thing in *his* loft." "Would
yer like me t'go up again?" asks Mary, afraid that the couple will
argue all night otherwise. "Oh, I *know* it's a nuisance, but could
you?" "I'll pop up there now." "Oh not tonight, dear, tomorrow,
when we've bought the rat-traps."

Unlike his confectioner son-in-law, Frank Kitchener *was* a fit
man over forty-five. More to the point, he considered himself
fit, and would have loved nothing better than to follow his sons
into the Flanders mire. Yet, his immediate duty was to carry on
providing for his wife and five, home-based children. The
combined weekly contributions made by Elisabeth and Louisa
were much appreciated, but they bore little relation to the considerable amount of food consumed by Frankie alone. Although
Lottie and Alice ate heartily, the boy's voracious appetite gave
credence to the old saying that within the stomach of every growing lad resides a wolf. And although Mary, Lillian, Gladys and
Sarah also contributed (the youngest daughters had recently
begun sewing work in one of the Queen's Work Centres), their
offerings were equally high in sentimental value but pitifully
insignificant financially. A man as devoted to his family as Frank
would never have enlisted under those circumstances. It was
perhaps fitting, therefore, that a compromise solution eventually
came from one of his dependants. It could not have come at a
better time: close on the heels of the saddest Christmas they had
ever experienced.

On Lady's instructions, the family table was laid as usual.
Places were thus set for Jack, Edward, Thomas, George and
Hubert. Most painfully of all, a place was also set for Mary, for
while there was still hope of seeing the boys alive, they knew that
they would never see Mary again. The tragic incident responsible
for this occurred in Christmas week itself. Providence had once

again contrived to bring misery to the family at what was supposed to be the happiest time of the year. Of course, Edward's disappointment over Alice's birth date; Frankie's broken arm, and Lady's infected finger now paled into insignificance. This was a savage blow. They had all been secretly steeling themselves for sorrowful news from the front, and it had crept up on them from whence it was least expected: Kensal Rise.

The traditional Christmas meal was eaten in respectful silence, each member of the Kitchener clan only too aware of the absentees eerily evoked at the table by their place settings. The following announcement two weeks later obviously came as a breath of fresh air: "Notice to Carpenters. About 200 wanted for sailing to France on February 20th to erect temporary hospitals – good wages." It was spotted in the local paper by Lady, who quickly foresaw the therapeutic benefits to be reaped by all were Frank to be accepted. Not only would it give vent to his pent-up desire to play an active role in the war, it would, moreover, serve to divert everyone's minds from the death of Mary and the possible deaths in action of the boys. However, shattered by the loss of his daughter, Frank at first showed no interest in the idea. "I'm too old, pet," he would claim with a weary sigh. But Lady was relentless in her efforts to persuade him that he should go. "Frank Kitchener, by the time this war's over we may have lost five of our sons. We may even have lost each other, but as long as there's breath in us we must do all we can to make sure we don't lose ourselves – our *real* selves, because the moment that happens then we're already as good as dead. Before...what happened to Mary, you'd have jumped at such a chance. Well jump at it now, 'cause now, more than ever, is when you need to. For *all* our sakes."

Thus pushed, he duly jumped. It was a 'decision' that did, indeed, prove beneficial to all concerned. Alas, its effects were to be tragically short-lived.

The prisoner under house-arrest lies fast asleep in his bed upstairs. He is sixty-seven year old Peter Rumbold, a jeweller by profession and a German by birth. Four large nails have been driven into a window frame to prevent a daring escape under cover of darkness. The bedroom door has been locked from the outside. SC Flanagan, who is doing the night shift with SC Laurence, even took the precaution of searching the prisoner for a glass-cutter, "wha' wiv 'im bein' a jeweller, know wha' I mean?" The two special constables keep vigil in the adjoining room, directly above the shop. Despite regulations to the contrary, Flanagan has lit a fire using the prisoner's coal.

"You're not really supposed to do that," Laurence feels obliged to say, even though he feels eternally grateful to his defiant colleague.

"Fing is they tell yer tha' cos they fink the cold keeps yer on yer toes. Far as I'm concerned, we ain' much use to no one frozen solid, know wha' I mean? 'Sides, it's 'is lot wha' star'ed this bleedin' war, so 'e can ruddy well pay t'keep us warm, can' 'e?"

After checking that the curtains are properly drawn, they pull up a couple of chairs and position themselves in front of the fire.

"Now this is wha' I call civilised," says Flanagan, resting his feet on a small ivory table. "Mine you, t'be hones' wiv yer, I'd rather be 'ome givin' the ol' wife some of tha'...(*gesticulating obscenely*) know wha' I mean? You married?"

"Yes," replies Laurence, drily.

"Don' know bou' you, bu' when I've gone withou' fer a few days, I jus' ain' meself, know wha' I mean? I feel all kine of res'less. Ge's so I'm practically doin' it, you know, in me 'ead, wiv every woman I see. Specially wiv them shor' skirts they're all wearin' nowadays. Never seen anyfink like it! They reckon it's cos there ain' 'nough material aroun' cos of the war. Blimey, in tha' case, le's 'ope it goes on a few more years, eh?"

"I think I'll just go and check the prisoner," says Laurence, rising to his feet.

"Check the prisoner? Wha' d'yer fink 'e 'is, a bleedin' magician or somink?"

"Better safe than sorry."

Flanagan takes the opportunity to down a swig of Scotch from his hip-flask. It makes sound economic sense to break some regulations in private. As he replaces the flask, it suddenly occurs to him that SC Laurence's overdevotion to duty, his nervous, fidgety air, smack of the telltale restlessness that he has just been describing. "Know them signs a mile off, I would... Course, wha' wiv 'im bein' a bit of an 'unchback, like, yer can 'ardly blame 'is missus, can yer?"

"Still there, is 'e?" he asks with a wry smile when Laurence returns.

"Fast asleep."

"Still, like yer said, bet'er safe than sorry... It's gonna be a long nigh' ain' it?"

"Yes. Why don't we take it in turns to sleep? I think it's silly for both of us to..."

"I've got a much bet'er idea." Flanagan lowers his voice. "There's a place not too far from 'ere where cer'ain ladies of the nigh' take their midnigh' constitutionals, know wha' I mean?"

"You're not seriously..."

"Why not? I could be back 'ere wiv one perched on each arm before yer could say Lloyd George."

Laurence is dumbfounded by the proposition. Why, it's pre-posterous, absurd. Ladies of the night, here, tonight... No! That wasn't the reason he'd become a special constable. But in spite of his reflex revulsion at the idea, the lewd seed that has been implanted in him begins to germinate. Overwhelming images of awesomely available women writhing amorously by the fire's side dart through his mind with spellbinding clarity. He wants des-perately to obliterate them, to tell himself that Flanagan is a lunatic, that he deserves to be expelled from the force for con-templating such a thing, but the lure of the multiplying images is gaining strength. Drawing on his reserves of self-control, he intersperses the visions of lithe-limbed damsels with glimpses of Elisabeth, but the memory of a swaying cross and diminutive, inaccessible golgothas only weakens his resolve. The temptation is now irresistible. He feels his mouth drying up while, in contrast, the palms of his hands grow moist. Rubbing the per-spiration on his trousers; swallowing hard; stooping low, he hears himself mumble, "We wouldn't be doing anyone any harm, I suppose."

Flanagan claps his hands. "Now yer talkin'! 'Ere, 'ave some of this. I save it for special occasions – an' don' say it ain' allowed. In fer a penny, in fer a poun', know wha' I mean?"

It was only a dream, but the vision of Elisabeth's bone-white cheeks; the blank, staring eyes; the hair brushed austerely off the face and arranged on the black-laced pillow like an open fan, shook Miss Dill to the core. Try as she might to convince herself otherwise, she knew, deep down, that her dream was no ordinary dream. She had dreamt too many premonitions in the past not to recognise its characteristic clarity of light and detail; its weight of foreboding. Not a word was said to Elisabeth about it (how could it be?), but in the wake of this experience, Miss Dill was surprised to discover in herself a budding, fatalistic concern for the future of Frankie. When, a week or so later, she asked Elisabeth if she would like to bring her nephew along with her occasionally, her answer was a resounding 'yes'. The suggestion was well-received for various reasons: it would provide Lady with a needy respite, herself with a travelling companion, and, most excitingly, it would re-introduce Frankie to the world of books. The large study was ideally suited to rekindling his interest. Fortunately for the child, however, Miss Dill held far less eccentric views on the subject of literary education – views which she wasted no time in communicating to him.

On his very first visit to the house, Miss Dill strode purposefully into the study, where Elisabeth was guiding the boy on a tour of the bound wonders on offer, and with a "Let's go out into the garden. It's snowing!", whisked Frankie off into the frozen paradise, where a length of swinging rope hung temptingly from an old oak branch. He could scarcely believe his eyes. "Well, what are you waiting for, young man?" she whispered in the boy's ear. Without further ado, Frankie sped towards it, leaving a trail of footprints and clouded breath in his wake. The twine felt as rugged and as hard as a rock when he tugged at it, a precautionary measure by one so young that impressed Miss Dill no end. The hearty tugs brought forth plaintive creaks from the overhanging branch, but obviously undaunted by these, and still holding onto the end of the rope, Frankie retraced his steps until there was no more slack left in it, then lunged forward again, skilfully positioning his feet on either side of a huge knot as he did so. The venture was a resounding success, and well-deserving of the applause it received from the two women. Not surprisingly, there followed numerous more swings, each a little more daring than the last. He swung and swung until his fingers were as raw and numb as Mary's in the scullery; until every single snowflake on the tree had been dislodged. But the best was still to come. There had to be a finale that was worthy of the rest of the performance, and he knew exactly what that entailed. "I'm jumping!" he announced, swinging into action for the last time. "Frankie, be careful!" cried Elisabeth from the warmth of the house. "Look, Libby!" he said, letting go of the rope in mid-flight. "Frankie!" "He's all right," Miss Dill assured her, gazing at her with a wistful fondness which Elisabeth misread as profound longing. "That's just how *I* used to come off the rope. See? What did I tell you?" Frankie skipped and smiled his way back to the house, waited until he was inside then shook the snow out of his hair and clothes with canine nonchalance.

"And remember," calls out Mrs Marshall as Mary disappears into the loft, "the springs have to be pulled right back. And don't put them all in one place. It's best to spread them out. You *will* mind your fingers, won't you, dear?"

Shivering with cold rather than fright (she knows full well that there are no rats or mice), she places and sets the lethal contraptions as instructed. Her actions are admittedly farcical, but at least they will buy some precious time in which to plan their next move. That it has gone on this long is as much a testimony to her guile and his endurance as it is to the good fortune that must currently be smiling on them. Yet luck, like any other vehicle, can be ridden only so far. Both of them are therefore quick to agree that alternative arrangements are well overdue. Negotiating the joists with consummate ease under the candle's glow, she makes for the wall that is farthermost from the trap-door. Now that she is up here, she might as well spend a few minutes with...

"Mary, dear!"

Everything happened so quickly. The startled spinning on heels to catch sight of Mrs Marshall's face in the loft entrance; the ensuing loss of balance amid high-pitched screams; the falling candle and the leaping, straw-fed flames; the caustic brightness daubing rafters and brickwork with orange hues; the hairy spectre in the corner that struck terror into the heart of Mrs Marshall before she plummeted, unconscious, to the floor below; the intense, all-engulfing, all-consuming heat; the panic of Victoria, who awoke to find smouldering debris raining down on her, and her bed covers ablaze; the safe escape of Mr Marshall and the children; the shocked expressions as they watched their home being devoured by the flames... In a little under half an hour, the building was a charred ruin. Only the efficiency of the fire-fighting services prevented the fire from spreading to the adjoining houses. Well into the new year, experts sieved in vain through the ashes in search of clues. Mr Marshall had been of little assistance, given that at the time he had been busy working in his surgery (that he made no mention of the straw in the loft and Mary's candlelit presence there can only be explained by the fact that he was in a state of shock). The boys were not much help either, although they each claimed to have heard their mother shout, "My God! Who on earth is that?" seconds before she fell (one of them was convinced she had actually said, "*What* on earth is that?"). However, despite the experts' failure to determine the precise cause of the blaze, they were, at least, able to rule out the harrowing possibility of arson. The unearthing of a pair of cracked boots which, inexplicably, had been the only objects to survive relatively unscathed, was deemed remarkable but of no consequence.

The two ladies of the night who had graciously interrupted their midnight constitutional to keep Flanagan and Laurence company during the long vigil are, in fact, nothing of the sort. The eldest is barely fourteen years old. Laurence, whose tantalising fantasies had so overwhelmed his better judgement, experienced an appreciable decline in his erotic appetite the moment he laid eyes on the girls.

Doing the right thing is suddenly a lot easier.

"Flanagan!" he protests, as his colleague sits one of the girls on his knee and proceeds to introduce the hip-flask into her mouth. "They're only girls!"

"Wha' d'yer expec', boys?"

Flanagan finds this so funny that he spills some whiskey down the girl's face. As he tries to lick it off, the younger of the two prostitutes ambles towards Mr Laurence. "Me an' Else are nice an' tigh'." She takes hold of his hand, but he yanks it free. "I'm clean, if tha's wha's troublin' yer."

"Flanagan! Take these girls back to where you found them – at once!"

Flanagan responds by pulling up the child's skirt and stroking her thigh.

"I'll report you!"

"Oh yeah? An' oo d'yer fink they're gonna believe? Me or you?"

"I don't care! This is despicable. You're *all* despicable!"

"In tha' case," remarks Flanagan, unbuttoning his trouser-buttons, "you'd bet'er wai' ou'side then, 'adn' yer? Cummon luv, there's plenny 'ere fer you too."

Laurence averts his gaze. What can he do? It would only be his word against Flanagan's. There would surely be an almighty scandal. Would he ever live it down? Albeit reluctantly, his doubts and the sound of derisory giggles and obscenities drive him towards the door.

"'Ang on!" cries Flanagan. "You ain' paid yer share ye'. No use changin' yer mine afterwards, is it?"

Without turning round, Laurence delves into his pocket, and tosses a few coins on the floor.

"Now there's a gen'leman!" remarks one of the prostitutes, running to pick up the money. "Sure yer don' wan' t'change yer mine?"

"Despicable!" mutters Laurence, opening the door.

The landing is cold and uncomfortable, but his born-again sense of righteousness would have it no other way.

Seven

Britannia ruled the waves. Dora ruled the land, but, in the modern world of the twentieth century, there was sadly no heroine to rule the sky. The glorious army regiments that had helped to build an empire could only stand and stare as enormous 650-feet long dirigible airships, filled with two million cubic feet of hydrogen, and carrying a weapon-load of twenty-seven tons, sailed menacingly overhead. These flying steeples, known popularly as 'Zepps', made their fearful presence felt in 1915. The distant rumble of their engines on a moonless night could reduce the populace to a gaping, quivering mass in seconds.

The Great Dora was truly powerless, but not for her the resort to gutless whines of "That's not cricket". No, having admitted her weaknesses, she did everything possible to thwart the largest German sausages that Britain had ever seen. Enforcing a blackout was a stroke of genius. Sadly, it was detrimental to national morale. Not easily discouraged (a sign of all great leaders and leaderenes), she turned to the noble hacks of Fleet Street. The thoroughfare was aptly named, for she had entrusted its workforce with no less than the dual role of minimising the effects of the enemy and raising the country's spirits, a role, of course, previously enacted by the Royal Navy. The response was immediate. For every bomb dropped from a Zeppelin, there were millions of centre-folds patriotically emblazoned with morale boosters like "German airmen are baby killers". Glaring inadequacies in the country's defences were ingeniously side-stepped by apportioning all blame to a mythical army of spies who were said to drive around the country on dark, overcast nights directing airships with "two powerful headlights".

Dora was elated. The same populace that had cowered under the mantle of darkness had been transformed into an incensed mob. Thanks entirely to the enterprising men of Fleet Street (inspired, one suspects, by the pioneering work of Ivan Pavlov), no self-respecting, God-fearing man, woman or child could fail to foam at the mouth when exposed to sounds like "Kaiser", "German" or "Hun". The hacks' subsequent reward for this was a place in the fast-growing government department at Wellington House.

It was only fitting that in this, the Greatest Show on Earth, the fantastic should play such a prominent role.

"Holy Father, remitter of our sins, please find it in your loving heart to forgive your Virgin Mother's namesake and rescue one so young and misguided from Lucifer's flames."

The nature of Mary's death had a profound effect on Elisabeth. Had she not predicted that her sister would burn in hell for writing those terrible letters? The fiery destruction of her body merely reflected the fate awaiting her soul. But she would never forsake her. Yes, Louisa had been so right: there *was* a wide gulf separating depravity from moral lassitude induced by love, or the desire for love. Her unspeakable feelings for a certain person meant that she was now in a position to understand that, so how could she possibly not have found it in her heart to forgive Mary and pray daily for her salvation when she herself yearned for similar compassion for *her* sins?

"That must be James," thinks Lady, hearing the familiar thud of the front door as her youngest son lets himself in.

James rushes up the stairs and into the kitchen, where his mother is in the middle of preparing a very important meal. He is panting and red in the face.

"Are they coming?"

"They weren' in," replies the boy, trying to catch his breath.

"Wasn't Ernest there? I know Elisabeth wouldn't be home yet..."

"No, bu' I left 'em a note."

"Oh, that was clever – well done."

"I go' some paper off a paper boy. I told 'em t'come 'ome straigh' away."

"Good," says Lady with an industrious sigh. "While I get on with this, you can play a bit with Lottie. She's been feeling rather sorry for herself today. Alice is still asleep." The lad screws up his face. "Please, James. I know she's little, but if you could just amuse her 'til the girls get home it would be a great help. I've a lot of preparing to do."

It is late evening by the time the Laurences arrive. The rest of the family have already been informed of the news, and there is an air of excitement in the house.

"We got the note," says Elisabeth, clearly fraught with worry. "Whatever's happened?"

"This!" answers her mother, holding up an unstamped envelope. "It got here today. It's from Jack!"

"From Jack!"

"At last," comments an out-of-uniform Mr Laurence.

"Oh, Frankie!" Elisabeth picks up her nephew, tears rolling down her cheeks. "A letter from Daddy!"

"Daddy! Daddy!" echoes the boy, half-expecting his father to emerge from the smiling ranks of relatives.

"What does it say?"

"We'd like you to read it out. It's addressed to all of us."

"D'you mean to say no one's read it yet?"

"Jack would want it this way, I'm sure."

Full of trepidation, Elisabeth takes the envelope. "This doesn't look like Jack's handwriting," she notes, surprised.

"It's signed by him, though," explains Lady.

"But I thought you said..."

"I only took a peep. I had to find out who it was from, didn't I?"

Expectant faces encircle Elisabeth as she carefully unfolds the letter. It is dated 30th January, 1915. The almost illegible scrawl is bespattered with mud and tea stains, and with the bold, black lines of His Majesty's censor. With trembling hands and voice, she begins to read,

"'My dear mother and father, brothers, sisters, little nieces, and dearest Frankie,

'You cannot imagine how much I am missing you all! I worry about you all of the time. There are rumours here of German bombings at home. I also know that you must be very worried about me too. I have tried writing many times before, but never managed it. I wrote a letter a few weeks after getting here, but went and lost it! I did not bother to write again after that because we all thought that we would be back by Christmas. Now we are not even sure if we shall be back by next Christmas, the way things are going. I suppose you want to know what things are like over here. The first few weeks were a bit rough, but I am used to it now, and it is not so bad. The crossing was a bit of a crush because we had to spend the night in horse-boxes. After docking at **XXXXX** we marched for days. None of us knew where we were going at first, but when we started hearing strange rumbles in the distance and seeing flashes of light, we knew that we were near the front. Once, they billeted us in a convent! We practised digging trenches all day in the rain! Not long after that, we reached the front, just as it started snowing! Our company has been split into platoons, and we take it in turns to man the trenches. Fred and I are in the same platoon. He has made lots of friends. It is not really dangerous in the trenches. Much of our time is taken up pumping away water and laying down planks. The other day one of the lads stopped one, but that was only because he was careless and stuck his head over the top. Sergeant **XXXXX** is always telling us to keep our heads down. They tell us that helmets are on their way but they are not an excuse for being careless. The hard work really starts at night. We have to see to the parapets or else they slide down. It is worse when it rains because the mud makes everything so slippery. There is nowhere for the water to go so it stays in the trench for days until we have pumped it all away. One night I had to go over the top to fill some water bottles from a shell hole. This is not really dangerous because the snipers cannot see you. The worst thing is the cold. The water in our bottles freezes up. We bivouac together for warmth. Our greatcoats were not much use once they got wet, so they gave us goatskin coats instead. You wear them with the hair on the outside! Before coming up the line we rub our feet with whale oil, but frost-bitten toes are still our biggest problem. After a few days in the trenches, it is back to our billets. Clean beds and clothes! Something funny happened the other day. We marched behind the lines to a brewery in **XXXXX** (I think that is how you spell it). There were these big vats full of hot water big enough for about ten men. It was my first hot bath since getting here! One of the lads noticed my nibbled toe and thought that it was frost-bite. I told him a rat had done it, and he said, "How did it get through your boot?" The trenches are full of rats, big fat ones. He could not believe it happened in London! While we were in the vats, they baked our uniforms in a big oven to kill off the lice.'"

"Kitchener!"

"Yessur!"

"Fall in!"

"Yessur!"

Seizing his Lee-Enfield, Private Kitchener asks his amanuensis (a man nursing a leg wound) to look after the letter until his return, and then joins a group of men who are waiting outside in torrential rain. Corporal Talbot is about to set off when he notices that Kitchener's right hand is heavily strapped. "You're no good to us like that – not on this mission."

"It's only sprained, Sir. I *can* fire with it."

He unravels the now sodden bandage.

"This is no bloody time for heroics! You shouldn't have volunteered, man!"

"It's all righ', really Sir."

Corporal Talbot prods him in the chest with his forefinger. "Grip that as hard as you can."

To the amusement of the three other privates, the non-commissioned digit is squeezed with such vigour that its owner is soon forced to order, "That'll do!"

French sentries salute heartily as the men pass through the courtyard of the large farmhouse where the company is billeted. The two platoons that will replace the two currently in the trenches left for the front several hours earlier. It is nightfall, and conditions underfoot are treacherous. Before very long, their progress is brought to a virtual standstill by a mixture of poor visibility and ankle-deep mud, but guided by the sound of field guns, they proceed as best they can towards the firing-line. Tonight, however, they will not be cutting across a familiar wood strewn with the decaying remains of horses, cattle, and the odd soldier. Instead, they will veer west, a bearing that should eventually lead them, undetected, to their chosen objective.

Every step is an impossible, endless descent into the un-known. In the unrelenting downpour, the mud is now up to their knees. As they wade through the liquid, chess-black earth, a voice is heard to utter, "Righ' bleedin' chocolate soldiers we are!" Even Corporal Talbot allows himself a smile. They are covered in clammy mud from head to toe. There is mud squelching inside their newly-issued gumboots, and mud sliding down the inside of their collars. Worse still, their saturated goatskins can offer no more resistance to the rain. Only their glinting bayonets have escaped contagion by the deepening morass. Yet, at times, the temptation to sink their rifles into the mire as a means of steady-ing themselves is great, but they know it must be resisted at all costs. They are, after all, infantry men, not gondoliers.

Original plans to take provisions, a Lewis-gun, and a boxful of magazine drums had to be ditched at the last moment as a result of the appalling weather conditions. Ironically, the mission has only gone ahead due to an inveterate faith in German efficiency.

It is another hour and a half before the ground becomes gravelly and easier to negotiate. Every now and then, it shakes as a volley of whizz-bangs explodes nearby. Mercifully, the rain has abated. They continue westward, parallel to their own tren-ches. Shortly, as expected, the mud disappears altogether. A gradual slope indicates that they have at last reached the rocky, crescent-shaped ridge that will take them to their target: a German sniper post. Corporal Talbot instructs his men to dis-mantle their weapons to ensure that they are still in working order. "Wouldn't be surprised if they've jammed solid," he states, sitting down. After their swampy ordeal, the feel of hard rock under their buttocks is a welcome relief. Minutes later, five shadowy figures resume their gradual ascent along the stony spine of the ridge. The elevated half-moon has soon carried them into no-man's-land, at which point it is deemed wise to complete what remains of their journey crawling on their bellies. In this position, the rugged terrain is no longer a source of comfort to them. With painful regularity, sharp protrusions embed themselves into elbows and knees. In the still of night, and between the sporadic explosions of shells, the softest utterance of complaint carries a perilously long way. Only too

aware of this, they grit their teeth and utter muted curse after
curse as the ground under them begins to steepen.

Each man has lost all track of time when the distinct sound of
German voices brings their progress to a sudden, welcome halt.
Corporal Talbot directs his men to stay where they are, then,
making as little noise as is humanly possible, he moves slowly
and stealthily towards the lip of a snipers' den perched on the
steepest part of the ridge. Judging from the Germans' chuckles,
they seem to be in good spirits despite the recent rain. After
listening intently to them, the corporal turns to his men and
holds up two fingers. Then he holds up one, indicating, with a
beckoning motion, that he wishes one of the men to join him.
Minutes later, when the man at his side has regained his breath,
Corporal Talbot holds up three fingers to him before mouthing
a silent, very deliberate countdown: *one...two...three*. On three,
they spring up like dolphins from the waves, their forearms
crashing down onto the sides of the dug-out – and it is all over.
Completely nonplussed, the two snipers stare wide-eyed at the
bayoneted rifles situated only inches from the frozen tips of their
noses. Instantly obeying the commands of gesticulating weapons,
they place their hands on their caps, and step out of the dug-
out. Corporal Talbot tells his man to escort them down to where
the remaining members of the party are waiting, and after
satisfying himself that there are sufficient provisions and ammu-
nition in the dug-out for at least another day (their faith was *not*
misplaced), he indicates to his men that he wishes three of them
to clamber up the rock-face. The three who do so are entrusted
with manning the post until they are relieved in twenty-four
hours. Having taken the position, it is vital to hold onto it – hence
the extra man. Kitchener and he will escort the Germans back
to the camp before returning to the trenches in the morning.
Wishing the privates luck, he takes his leave of them and scampers down the incline.

Their rifles are trained on enemy backs. Although there has
been no rain for some hours, the return trek to the farmhouse is
no less formidable. In many parts, the mud is still knee-deep, so
their concentration has to be equally divided between keeping
their balance and keeping the Germans in their sights. There is

no room for error: literally one slip and the mission could easily be ruined.

Strangely, considering how late it is, the first Verey rocket of the night lights up the sky, throwing its silvery glare over four shivering, precariously-balanced soldiers. Two of these take the opportunity to gaze round at their captors, who are more than a little surprised to discover that their prisoners are extremely young. Jelly-babies doing a chocolate soldier's job. No wonder it was so easy to dislodge them. As the level of mud and corresponding fear of slipping gradually subsides, the blades of their bayonets cut a slow, upward arc, barrels finally coming to rest on their shoulders.

Was it complacency or sheer exhaustion that made them aim distractedly at the nigrescent clouds? Perhaps it was both, which would explain why Corporal Talbot, with all his experience, fell for the old trick of the prisoner who, suddenly clutching his stomach, crumples awkwardly to the ground, where he twists and turns while uttering a string of plaintive cries. As he stood over the writhing youth, inquiring, in pidgin German, if he was all right, the other youth dealt him a bludgeoning blow to the side of the head which sent him tumbling to the ground. Kitchener, who had not contemplated such an eventuality, fumbled for his Lee-Enfield as the prostrate sniper tugged desperately at the rifle trapped under the corporal. Fearing for his life; convinced that they had killed Corporal Talbot, Kitchener fired a deafening shot at the upright and more accessible of the two prisoners, who, as startled birds noisily abandoned their roosts, staggered back several feet before his legs buckled and he collapsed in a heap. Petrified by the blast, the remaining youth lay motionless, his hands clasped around the barrel of the rifle. Tight-lipped and in a deep state of shock, Kitchener advanced towards him, bayonet thrust out menacingly. Sensing his intentions, the lad gave up on the rifle, rose slowly to his feet and placed his hands on his head. Each and every sinew in his panic-stricken body was pleading to be spared, but the steely tip drew closer and closer. The young man, his face taut with terror, sank to his knees and pronounced a Teutonic "No!" which made not the slightest impact on the Englishman. Clamping his eyes shut for the last time, he braced himself for the inevitable, cold stab of pain. It was at that precise moment in time that Private J.S. Kitchener of the 9th Battalion Middlesex Regiment glanced up and saw his wife.

The eyes inherited by her son were no longer taking him in with an impassive serenity. They were imbued with love once again, and the cheeks that had slowly drained of colour until they were ashen were rosier than they had ever been. There were no Vereys overhead, and yet Jack could see her perfectly. It was as if *she* were giving off light.

"Rose!"

The German, who was still bracing himself for the final, violent lunge, prised open an eyelid. The bayonet loomed over his heart. To his horror, the soldier with the strange expression was sadistically delaying the moment of execution. He started sobbing like a child.

"Rose!" repeated Jack, totally oblivious to his prey.

After years of trying to come to terms with her death, it was perfectly obvious that she was alive and well.

"Don' 'urt 'im, Jack."

Her words rang out clearly, but her lips, he was certain, had not moved.

"Rose!"

She stretched out a hand, and as she did so, the radiant glow around her, and from her, began to weaken.

"If you love me, Jack, you'll also stop torturin' yerself..."

"Rose!"

"We'll be together again one day, bu' you mus' le' go of me 'til then... I have to...go...now..."

She was gone. The luminous apparition was swallowed up by darkness, and as he stared, transfixed, at the empty space where she had stood, or hovered, the tears coursed down his face. He was on the verge of calling out her name once more when he heard sobs, and came to as though from a trance. The young German was crying relentlessly, and Jack suddenly became aware of his own tears. He was wiping his face when Corporal Talbot stirred.

"Sir!"

"Not so loud!" he moaned, rubbing the side of his head. Struggling to his feet, he added, "What a damn fool I was."

"They took us by surprise, Sir. I sho' one of 'em."

"Poor stupid bastard...It's only when you see them lying dead like that that you remember they've got mothers and fathers... We'll come back in the morning and bury him. Ouch, my head! I haven't been hit that hard since I went in the ring with an old pro down in Dorset."

"I though' you were..." Kitchener refrained from saying the obvious word out of an odd sense of respect. "You know..."

"It'll take a lot more than that to stop me seeing my wife and little girl again, I can tell you. It's what keeps us *all* going, isn't it?"

Kitchener nodded, the ironies of the remark not lost on him. And what ironies! The blow that almost killed the corporal and his hopes of seeing his loved ones again was the same blow that had led to Rose returning from the dead! And to have been reunited with his Rose *here*, of all places: in the land of poppies! To have seen her blooming as never before in a soil treated with chloride of lime to lessen the stench of putrefying flesh! To have taken a vital step towards a full acceptance of her death as a result of seeing her so full of life!

An hour or so later, a bleary-eyed Gordon Highlander salutes the mud-caked trio as they enter the confines of the farmhouse. Other, less trusting sentries halt them in their tracks, bellowing, "Who goes there?", to which a flinching corporal invariably retorts, "Not so loud!" In the early morning gloom, the farmhouse roof appears to rise and fall to the sound of hundreds of snoring men. Only a few officers are to be seen milling around outside.

"Get out of those wet clothes, Kitchener. I have to report back to Major Alderman."

"Yes, Sir. Wha' abou' '*im*?"

"He's coming with me. I fancy our lot would like a few words with him. Oh, and, er, I think the less said about that little episode back there the better."

"Yes, Sir."

Kitchener crossed the courtyard and entered a large barn.

He filled an old bucket that hung suspended from a standpipe, and stripped off. Despite the numbing cold, it was a relief to part company with his heavy, water-laden coat and uniform. To his amazement, he found that he was also a chocolate soldier in the flesh. Teeth chattering, he stepped into the bucket and sluiced as much water over himself as he could. Dark brown rivulets rolled down his trembling torso. Mistaking the clots of blood around his elbows and knees for dirt, he rubbed at them until they bled. Three bucketfuls later, he collected his muddy clothes and hastened to the warmth of the farmhouse. Leaving the soggy bundle by the foot of his bed, he climbed in and, within minutes, had sunk into a sleepy quagmire.

"Kitchener! Wake up!"

The dormant mass stirred, mumbled a few incomprehensible words, but did not surface from its slumber.

"Kitchener!"

"Wha'!" he cried with a start.

"Sshhh! You'll wake everyone up."

It was Corporal Talbot.

"Sir!"

"Listen. The major was so pleased with the success of the mission, he's given me the next eight hours to myself, no questions asked. I managed to get the same for you. So hurry up and get dressed."

"Dressed? But Sir, all I wan'a do is sleep."

"You'll sleep, all right, but not here. Come on, you're wasting time."

"But my clothes, they're all..."

"I've taken care of that. Here, put these on."

"But where we goin'?" he asked, reluctantly pulling back the bedclothes.

The corporal frowned. "Armentières, if you must know, but didn't anyone ever tell you never to stare a gift horse in the mouth?"

At a brisk pace, they reached the town in just under three quarters of an hour. Along the way, a soft, golden halo intensified the barren starkness of silhouetted trees, and the violent exchanges of field guns in the distant front were reduced by the intervening morning air to a cantankerous altercation between a couple of old fuddy-duddies.

Despite feeling deliriously tired at the outset, Jack was rapidly invigorated by the walk. However, the balmy contact of dry clothes on his skin was a constant reminder of the warm bed he had left behind. Not wishing to be accused again of staring a gift horse in the mouth, he refrained from making any further queries. Since neither man was much given to small-talk, there was therefore little opportunity to glean any clues as to the nature of the gift awaiting him. As they walked in silence on the blissfully mud-free road to Armentières, he could at least take comfort in the fact that the brightening sky augured no rain.

In marked contrast with its outskirts, which curled around it like a cat, the centre of Armentières was throbbing with activity even at that early hour. Military vehicles of all descriptions, including requisitioned ambulances bound either for Boulogne or the front, were in evidence everywhere. Large groups of gregarious women waited outside every provisions shop. As the two soldiers edged past them, they were enthusiastically saluted, even by the many holding blanketed infants in their arms.

"This is the one," said Corporal Talbot, turning into a small side-street.

When they came upon a house with a grey, dilapidated façade, he took Kitchener by the arm and led him into a doorway. Much to the private's surprise, his superior banged on the door with a vehemence that belied the hour of day.

"Won' yer friens mind bein' woken up at this time, Sir?" he asked, anxiously.

"I wouldn't worry about my friends if I were you. They keep an open house. They're always glad to see you here. Ah, there we are!" he added, as a bolt was drawn back.

The door opened to reveal an ageing woman in a dressing-gown. Unsmiling, she bowed her head, stepped to one side and pointed up the stairway behind her. Rather baffled, Kitchener followed the corporal inside and up to the first floor, where they were shortly joined by the woman who had let them in. This time she waved her hand in the direction of a door at the end of a long, gloomy corridor before continuing her ascent to the second floor. The room where, presumably, they were to wait for her contained a single piece of furniture: a well-worn divan. Strewn across the floorboards was a threadbare collection of rugs, while old sheets nailed to the window-frame doubled as curtains.

"Who was tha' woman, Sir?"

"Her name's Madame La Fontaine."

"Who is she?"

"She owns the place."

Kitchener, who had removed his greatcoat on entering the house, was forced to put it on again. He stood up and walked around the shabby room, arms clasped together. "Freezin', ain' it, Sir?" he said.

"Not for long it won't be," came the cryptic reply. Hearing footsteps outside, he added, "You'd better sit down. I think they're coming."

"They?" he thought, joining the corporal on the divan. As predicted, the owner of the house did not return alone: she was accompanied by five other women of varying age who had clearly just been roused from their sleep. They lined up dutifully in front of the men, and when Madame La Fontaine clapped her hands, uttering a weary "Messieurs, voilà!", the sundry quintet displayed their goose-skinned wares with professional synchronicity. Regardless of the general disparity in stature, each pair of thighs and every midriff was a mass of thick, drooping folds. Only their breasts, a pendulous mixture of firmness and flaccidity, displayed patent differences.

Kitchener was dumbstruck. By anyone's standards, it had been an eventful night. He had waded through oceans of liquid earth; crawled over stony ground littered with rocks; played an admittedly minor part in taking an enemy position; shot a man; almost bayoneted another; seen his dead wife, and now this: a veritable herd of gift horses inviting him to stare into every conceivable opening.

"Messieurs?"

"Which one do you fancy?" asked Corporal Talbot, prodding him in the ribs with his elbow.

He remembered the blooming, thriving spectre...the words it had spoken. Sensing that his silence had something to do with a naive concern for the sanctity of marriage vows, the corporal remarked, confidentially,

"Look, no one cares more about their wife than I do, but let's face it: you and I could be pushing up daisies this time next week."

Daisies, poppies, roses...a heady combination of scents which mingled with the women's pungent perfume and infused him with a profound sense of peace and well-being.

And so it was that, in accordance with her obvious wishes, Rose Kitchener's death was finally consummated on the banks of the River Lys.

"This part's dated the 2nd of February," Elisabeth informs them. "'Cannot tell you much about it, but I took part in an important mission last week. It was very exciting, and one day I hope to tell you all about it. Heard today that Fred is up for an Albert Medal! I am very happy for him. We are off to the front again tomorrow. We have been having quite good weather recently (makes a change!) so it should not be too bad in the trenches. I have no way of knowing anything about Edward, George, Hubert and Thomas, but I hope you have heard from them and that they are as well as I am. You can write to me at the special address on the envelope. All the boys here are fond of a ciggie or two but as there are never enough to go round, they would appreciate it very much if you could send some when you write. Must stop now.

'Please do not worry about me. I am in very good spirits and quite enjoying myself. I am sure it will not be long before I see you all again.

'All my love, Jack.

'P.S. You must be wondering why I have not written this letter myself. It is because I sprained my hand the other day pumping out the trenches. My writing was never any good anyway, so it was a good excuse to get somebody else to do it for me! His name is Denis, by the way, and he sends his regards.'" Elisabeth looks up and sighs. "What a relief to know he's all right!"

"I think we should toast to him and all the boys," suggests Lady, raising her glass. "To Jack, Edward, Thomas, Hubert and George!"

"God bless 'em!" cries Frank. "An' Fred, le's no' forge' 'im!"

Glasses are duly tilted, after which Lady clears her throat as though she has something important to announce. "There's another reason why I wanted us to eat together tonight." She places an arm around her husband. "Frank's leaving for France next week, and I thought it would be nice if we..."

"That's a lovely idea!" exclaims Elisabeth, still clutching Jack's letter.

"To Mr Kitchener!" calls out Mr Laurence, his drinking arm aloft.

Eight

"Set your face resolutely against the worst enemy that this country has, not the German, but the pacifist, the peacemonger, who would barter your birthright, your liberty and your honour, as well as the country's welfare, for the sake of a cheap and worthless peace. Better that the country should fight to the last until nothing is left than have that peace which would give Germany the power of renewing this terrible conflict a few years hence. If we love our country we are bound to fight to the very end until this horrible danger which has hung over Europe for so many years has been totally destroyed, so that those who come after, may live in peace and quiet... Let us pray."

The congregation kneels.

"Our Father..."

The Watch Night service is drawing to a close.

"...Thy will be done..."

The Rev. George Martin's words have had a balsamic effect on troubled souls.

"Amen."

The congregation rises. St John's, Kilburn, empties. Outside, the rain continues to fall.

The years, like the battles, have come and gone. Mons, Marne, Somme, Gallipoli, Ypres...

Yes, the Western Front run is breaking all records, and although there is a high turnover of supporting players, the leading parts, save one very important exception, are still being enacted by the same household names. (It is with great regret that we inform our patrons of the loss of the Secretary of State for War, who drowned on the 5th of June, 1916, when the cruiser

'Hampshire' struck a German mine. Though it will always be associated with him, his part will be performed by Mr David Lloyd George for the foreseeable future.) But despite the fact that the aforementioned Mr Lloyd George is now Prime Minister; that votes for suffragettes-cum-munitionettes-cum-Wrafs and Waacs and Wrens are just around the parliamentary corner; that universal conscription, as foretold by Mr Laurence, has been introduced (creating a phenomenon known as a conscientious objector – the "little piggy who stayed at home"); that the Americans have finally nailed their stars and stripes to the Allies' mast, not a great deal has changed in the past three years. It is a question of degree: tighter belts, even shorter skirts, longer queues, more allotments, less food, more blackouts and restrictions on shop lighting, longer obituary columns, more absentees, more anti-German riots...

Dora, however, merits special mention. Politics' answer to Florence Nightingale, the undisputed custodian of the nation's welfare, she has gone from strength to strength, or at least she is convinced she has. It is all too easy to say, as her growing number of critics are intimating, that her absolute powers have gone to her head. Dora certainly has unlimited powers, yet is it unreasonable of her to outlaw (1) discussing naval and military matters in public places; (2) spreading rumours concerning military affairs; (3) trespassing on railways and bridges; (4) using codes when writing overseas; (5) lighting bonfires; (6) flying kites; (7) purchasing binoculars; (8) melting down gold or silver; (9) feeding bread to dogs, poultry or horses, and (10) saying anything offensive about British or Allied Forces? Is it unreasonable or is it an enlightened manifestation of a zealous patriot who dare not underestimate the deviousness of her foes?

Alas, great leaders and performers are all too often at the evaluating mercy of lesser minds. Despite her undoubtedly honourable and selfless intentions, Dora is no more the apple of everyone's eye. The hearts and imaginations of modern palacegoers have been captured by a certain Mary Pickford. Clearly perturbed by the fickleness of a once adoring public, the everfaithful doyens of Wellington House are entrusted with the task of instilling a sense of strict discipline into each and every citizen. Fickleness does not win wars. They are their own worst enemies because of it. A doyen gasps, raising a finger to the heavens. "That's it!" The others gather round. "Their own worst enemies ... Forget the child-eating Hun. There is another, ultimately more dangerous enemy in our midst: the bread-eating Briton!" Shrewd smiles of acknowledgement extend slowly as the idea sinks in. Someone cries, "England Expects Economy!" and without further ado, the script-writers rush to their desks. "I like that," thinks Dora. "The three E's." The industrious sound of scratching nibs is music to her ears. By the end of the evening, they are ready to present their wares. "Eat less bread and victory is secure." Dora nods approvingly. "Look well at the loaf on your breakfast table and treat it as if it were real gold because that British loaf is going to beat the German... Today the kitchen is the key to victory and is in the fighting line alongside our undying heroes of the trenches." Dora kisses the wise brow, which is liberally coated with perspiration. And then, the masterpiece: "I am a slice of Bread. I am wasted once a day by 48,000,000 people of Britain. I am 'the bit left over'; the slice eaten absent-mindedly when really I wasn't needed: I am the waste crust. If you collected me and my companions for a whole week you would find that we amounted to 9380 tons of good bread – WASTED! SAVE ME, AND I WILL SAVE YOU!" Dora, already aroused by the taste of salt upon her full lips, steps forward and takes the master by his unsullied hand. The others stand aside in awe as the intertwined couple stride sweetly towards the privacy of an adjoining room.

Such are the ways of jilted stars and understanding doyens.

News of George and Hubert came in the spring of 1915, even though they had actually frozen to death in the winter. The Kitcheners had lost a daughter in a blaze, and now the cold had claimed two of their sons. As fate would have it, Frank, who had returned from France with rediscovered vigour, arrived home on the very day that the tragic news was broken to the family. He was inconsolable, and even Lady, the clan's seemingly endless source of strength and courage, plunged into a deep depression and had to be confined to her bed, where she would wail hysterically for hours at a time. This cruel, bitter blow, or rather the devastating effects it had on her parents, presented Elisabeth with the perfect opportunity to escape the house above the sweet-shop (her worst fears had indeed been realised by then), but not even she could have realised how permanent her move was destined to be as she rolled up her sleeves and took over her mother's duties.

Whereas Mary's death had bolstered Louisa's resolve, persuading her of the need to carry on gritting her teeth in the face of adversity (she could have gone on indefinitely enduring the Fowler's petty antipathy against her), the deaths of George and Hubert were too close for comfort. Far too close. They had lost their lives on the same, horrible front where Edward... Naturally, she had always worried about him, but had never seriously contemplated the thought of losing him. He would be back one day. Of course he would. He had a wife and two daughters to return to. He couldn't possibly... The stark realities of war had been brought home to her with a resounding death knell. What did she care about Belgium, bits of paper (international currency or not), and evil Kaisers? The only thing she wanted – the only thing that every single wife, mother and child wanted was HIS safe return. In the space of a few days, the attractive servant girl had acquired strange, bulbous protuberances around the eyes, and deep lines had formed where earlier only the softest of shadows had been. Her plight touched even the hearts of the Fowlers. Before them was no longer a hardy gritter of teeth to be despised and reviled. Subservient teeth were now being gnashed in a distressed and, above all, endearing admission of vulnerability. Mrs Fowler was the first to warm to her (under the circumstances, it could hardly have been her husband).

It might, perhaps, be uncharitable to suggest that it was Louisa's physical deterioration rather than her obvious distress that prompted Mrs Fowler to express genuine concern. But whatever her motives, show genuine concern she did. Her unexpected transformation was rendered complete when she encouraged Mr Fowler to "be a little more considerate with Louisa". The arduous, often demeaning chores to which she had been subjected in the wake of *the incident* were soon replaced by hours of soothing inactivity, during which the three of them would sit around the kitchen table sipping hot cups of coffee (tea was as hard to come by as bread, sugar, margarine and coal).

"I'm sure you'll soon hear from him again," Mrs Fowler assures her.

"I know I shouldn' fre' so much, but..."

"We understand. It's only natural... How's Mrs Kitchener now?"

"She's no' a shadow of 'er old self."

"After what that poor woman's been through, I'm not surprised," remarks Mr Fowler gravely.

"Libby's been takin' care of 'em an' my lit'le Lot'ie an' Alice. She's an angel, Libby is. Gave up 'er job for a week an' everythin'."

"Oh dear," sighs Mrs Fowler, feeling the pot to see whether it is still hot. "I do hope this awful war's over soon."

When, several months later, sad tidings of Thomas' death reached his already grieving family (*It is with great regret...was killed serving his...did you, his regiment and his country proud...*), it seemed only a matter of time before the same fate befell Jack and Edward. As if bracing themselves for the inevitable, they began speaking about the two surviving brothers in the past tense.

The fresh loss had two important consequences. It provided Elisabeth (*and* Mr Laurence, who was for ever being asked by neighbours about the whereabouts of his wife) with a credible pretext for staying on longer at her parents' home. Ironically, the second consequence directly undermined this pretext, for, unable to tap new reserves of grief with which to fuel her present sorrow, Lady found herself indulging less and less in her mournful malaise. Gradually, she recaptured her former determination, and was soon rebuking those around her who failed to refer to Jack and Edward in the present tense. Frank, who had not only been grieving the death of three of his sons but the living-death of the woman he had married and relied so heavily on, took heart when it became apparent that her old self had risen like a Phoenix out of the ashes.

During the modest Christmas repast of 1915 (Elisabeth had dissuaded her mother from setting a place for the deceased and absent), Lady delivered one of her famous, impromptu speeches.

"Christ said 'Give unto Caesar what is Caesar's, and give unto God what is God's', or something like that. Well, this is what I think we should do, all of us, as a family: give death..." pausing painfully, as if the words are stuck in her gullet, "Mary, George, Hubert, Thomas...what is death's, and give life what is life's. By all means let's mourn them, but let's not forget to pray for those who are still alive, to think of them that way. That's the least we can do for Jack and Edward."

It goes without saying that no mention of their siblings' deaths was made in any of their correspondence with them.

The picture of a helpless man hung helplessly over a helpless woman. She too looked up in anguish and wondered why he had forsaken her. She too had known of her torment in advance. She too refrained from fighting back.

The Ecce Homo above the bed witnessed it all.

Would it have happened if Flanagan had not acted as he did? We shall never know, of course. The most probable explanation seems to be that, slowly but surely, SC Laurence's intitial reaction of righteousness dissolved into an insidious sense of loss, and that explicit images of alluring sirens bearing no relation to the reality of the two girl prostitutes returned to haunt him. What harm could it possibly have done? Such deliberations, one suspects, became obsessive. It is not difficult to imagine the good constable, his mind a tantalising harem of idealised seduction, having to relieve himself two, three, maybe even four times in the course of his special duties. And the ensuing shame; the guilt; the glimmer of righteousness, followed, as always, by the enslaving visions of desire. Eventually, no doubt, the method of inducing his short-lived periods of relief grew less appealing as it grew more ineffective. It must have been around this time (a month or so after the receipt of Jack's first letter) that he began to yearn for a more gratifying means of release from his tormentors, and that the word 'tight' came to sodomitical prominence in his thoughts.

Yes, in the dark of night, the Ecce Homo witnessed it all. Witnessed the furtive ogling; felt the electric charge in the air as a succession of awkward advances were silently repulsed; heard the bed moan under a violently-shifting weight; observed the martyred look before and after she was slapped about the face and forced to lie on her front; watched the covetous veneration of parted buttocks, and seen, heard, felt the initially careful, ultimately frenzied execution of a haunting obsession.

Unable to turn a blind eye, the overhanging deity contemplated the ensuing shame; the guilt; the glimmer of righteousness... No stranger to the phenomenon of transfiguration, the figure on the wall viewed with impassivity the bewildered, frightened and repentant expression of a man wondering what could possibly have possessed him.

A broken marriage had been de-consummated in and under the eyes of God.

Only Miss Dill was made privy to what had happened. "...and then he..."

Elisabeth breaks down. She has been on the verge of it ever since she began. Caring, comforting arms embrace her. An understanding bosom provides a soothing refuge. Sympathetic fingers caress a moist cheek once lined with blood. "That's it," whispers a voice by her ear. "That's it... Let it all out... You'll feel much better for it."

"Oh Emmy, what I am going to do?"

"Don't worry," cheek upon cheek, "everything's going to be all right. Just you wait and see." A kindly kiss. "You have to think of Frankie."

"Oh yes, I know," sniffing, trying to compose herself. "Last night, if it hadn't been for Frankie I would have punched and kicked and ..."

Fresh tears...a fresh embrace.

Florence Welch, aged fifteen, and her brother Alexander, two years her junior, were charged with breaking into a gas meter, and spending the proceeds of the theft, 12s., on sweets (had all juveniles been this enterprising, a certain trader might never have been forced to shut up shop). Florence, a munitions worker, was sent to a place of detention for fourteen days.

There is no doubting it: the criminal mind is considerably harder to prise open than any safe or gas meter. That one contemplates its perverse workings with a sense of social outrage is not to be doubted either. After all, what would societies come to if the tiny minority who shun the laws of democratically-elected chambers were applauded by the vast majority? Felonies of every description would rapidly become the lauded order of the day.

The crimes most abhorred by states, churches, and peoples alike (ranging from homicide to genocide) would draw the largest crowds, earn the highest acclaim. However, the fact remains that the perverse workings of the criminal mind are also contemplated with the sort of chilling fascination with which one contemplates a deadly snake – no, more so, for no one expects to find a drop of human kindness in a cold-blooded reptile, but to peer into a person's face and discover that every conceivable facet associated with the reprehensible is in a state of shameless exaltation is truly terrifying. Or is it actually the secret longing to savour this ruthless inconformity that one finds so chilling? If so, does it follow that the greater the social outrage, the greater the secret admiration (that we are, so to speak, judging and condemning ourselves)? Is this true of governments and counsels for the prosecution as well?

The relative harshness of the punishment inflicted upon young Florence and Alexander would appear to uphold this theory. (The learned counsel for the defence rises.) ... M'lud, I will, if I may, bring to the attention of the jury what we believe to be the crux of this case. What, I ask you, honourable members of the jury, are we trying? You will note that I did not ask you *whom* are we trying, and herein, we believe, lies the unusualness of this case. As far as we are concerned, it is the defendants who are on trial, albeit for a crime that we do not deny they committed, but it has not escaped our notice, as I trust it has not escaped yours, that the prosecution have, for the most part, concentrated on how, nay on *what* the modest fruits of the crime were spent. And this, members of the jury, raises serious legal as well as moral questions, because I dare say that had the defendants used the proceeds of their crime to finance a visit to, say, a local cinema showing *The Daughter of the Gods*, in which, I believe, over 19,000 people and 5,000 horses appear in one scene, and had they treated their ageing mother to this remarkable spectacle, I very much doubt whether the manifest wrath of the prosecution would have been incurred. I even go so far as to say that had the defendants tampered with a dozen meters in order to buy some National War Bonds, they would have been swamped with praise by all concerned. But you need no reminding that they spent their ill-got profits on procuring sweets for themselves. Yes, honourable members of the jury, sweets. An innocent and common enough practice on the face of it, and something at which not even the prosecution would normally take umbrage. But the key word is 'normally', and, as all of us are only too aware, these are anything but normal times. The war is into its fourth year, and though an end to the unprecedented carnage of suffering seems closer than it has ever done, the fact still remains that the blockade around our shores by enemy submarines has led to massive shortages of supplies in our shops, and there is, at the present moment, nothing in less supply and greater demand than sugar. Yes, sugar, the stuff of which sweets are made. M'lud, members of the jury, it is our considered contention that the nature of the prosecution's attack and the reason why they are pressing for such severe sentences, coming, as it does, close on the heels of the Food Controller's announcement that the sugar ration is to be fixed at half a pound, is linked, inextricably and, we think, unjustifiably, to a thinly veiled desire to set an example to all potential violaters of the Controller's regulations. There is absolutely no doubt whatsoever in our minds that our learned colleagues for the Crown have limited themselves to what they construe as an audacious and unpatriotic flaunting of emergency laws introduced under the Defence of the Realm Act. This is arrant nonsense! Corrosive that they are, these sweets seem to have struck a nerve, bringing into play a whole series of painful repressions. I urge the jury to address itself to the crime and nothing but the crime. It is the petty, and I stress, petty theft of money from a gas meter that you are being asked to consider, and not, by any stretch of the imagination, whether the use to which it was subsequently put constitutes a symbolic defiance of the government's rationing policy. A man who rides to church on a stolen nag is no less a horse-thief than a man who steals a mount to ride to a brothel. In the blindfolded eyes of the Law, both men are equally guilty of the crime, and will therefore suffer the same punishment. It cannot be emphasized too strongly: we are not about the judicial business of reading into crimes whatever happens to suit our personal or political ends... (Sweeping back his robes, the counsel for the defence sits down.)

Frank L. Kitchener, aged six and a half, will not be charged with anything (and therefore will not require the services of our examplary, if imaginary, barrister). The grand sum of 2/9 in his possession has been acquired through sheer honest endeavour. Admittedly, he may never have thought of it himself, but once alerted by his friend Jim to the financial rewards to be had, he set about the task with dogged determination.

It had all started with an advertisement in the local press selected at random by Elisabeth for her daily reading class with Frankie: "Waste Paper Wanted for Munitions – Sell every bit at top prices to Alex. L. Dribbel, 84 Carlisle St, Edgware Road, N.W.8. Vans collect Daily – Sack supplied Free of Charge." Jim, who was waiting patiently for his friend to finish his dreaded lesson, cocked his ears. "Miss Libby. Me an' Frankie coul' do tha'."

"What?" asked Frankie, who had been concentrating so hard on trying to match the right sound to the symbols before him that their meaning had quite escaped him.

Elisabeth smiled. "Of course you could! I think it's an excellent idea."

Two days later, each boy was presented with a large sack. It was agreed that they should begin their search next door, where Jim lived with his widowed mother (a munitionette). When they returned to the Kitchener household, Elisabeth was surprised to see them looking so disgruntled.

"What ever's the matter?"

"Didn' find much," complained Frankie.

She glanced at the diminutive bulges in their sacks. "You mustn't give up that easily. I'm sure you'll find plenty here." However, a few bits of cardboard and the odd newspaper later, they repeated their frowned complaint to Elisabeth, who was just about to leave for Hampstead. "Oh dear, I thought there'd be much more than that to collect. Now, let me see." She rummaged through her coat-pockets and produced a list that Mr Dribbel himself had given her. "The best things to collect are newspapers. For every pound you get 1 1/4d. Next best are ledgers and account books at a penny per pound... I know just the place."

The pavements of High Road Kilburn have disappeared under a mass of people. The few who are not queuing for their allotted ration of food are forced to walk along the fringes of the busy road. All of a sudden, a cry rings out, and a woman wrapped in an old blanket falls to the ground in the path of Elisabeth and the boys. Elisabeth helps her to her feet, but she shows no inclination to return to the queue. "Are you all right?" she calls out as the woman moves aimlessly away. "I'm sure they'll let you back in the queue." "Over our dead bodies!" snaps the queue. "'er son's a C.O." Elisabeth looks puzzled. "A conscientious objector!" "But surely that's no..." The angry viper spits its venom. Holding back the tears, Elisabeth wipes away the sputum from the bridge of her nose. "It's the likes of you wha' encourages 'em!" Unbeknown to her, the two boys retaliate by sticking out their tongues just before she leads them across the road.

"What a pleasant surprise!" says a sleepy-eyed Mr Laurence, joining them downstairs in the shop. "I've been on night-duty, that's why... But never mind about me. Hello, Frankie! Is this a friend of yours?"

"Yes."

"And what's your name?"

"Jim," comes the coy reply.

"Hello Jim... Hello," he adds, turning to Elisabeth for the first time.

"Hello Ernest."

They have hardly spoken to each other since...

"Well, I *am* glad you dropped in. You two look like a pair of Father Christmases with those sacks."

"Ernest, I must be off soon. Emmy'll be wondering what's happened to me."

"Yes, yes of course. You run along, I'll look after these two."

"Is the stock room still full of your old books?"

"Why yes. I'll say it is. I've been meaning to burn the lot for years."

"Burn 'em!" cries Frankie. "We're gonna sell 'em!"

"They're needed for munitions," explains Elisabeth.

"Oh, I see. Yes, of course they are. How silly of me. And that's what those sacks are for, right?"

The boys nod their heads with eager anticipation.

"Can I leave them with you 'til this evening?"

"Of course you can."

Elisabeth allows a fleeting look to pass between them. "Thank you."

"How's...Lady?" he inquires a little too eagerly.

"She's getting stronger, but...you know what the doctor said."

"Yes," he answers a little too disappointed.

Realising that no one mourns or remains in a state of depression indefinitely, Elisabeth had been forced to pretend to her husband that Lady had been diagnosed as having "a weak heart", and that nobody but she had been made privy to the fact because "the others would worry themselves sick." A different subterfuge had to be deployed to explain to her mother why she showed no desire to return to her own home. "Ernest insists I stay," she lied. "He says that if you can put up with everything you've had to put up with, plus the constant dread of *more* tragic news arriving at any time, then he can put up with living alone until the war's over – and he won't have it any other way. He knows how much needs to be done here, and you're not getting any younger, Mum."

"Goodbye."

"I'll have a cup of tea waiting for you when you get back," promises Mr Laurence.

Smiling more dutifully than gratefully, she turns to the youngsters and gives them a big hug. "Happy collecting!"

Blissful collecting would have been more accurate. Ah...the stock room! A fantastic mine of ledgers dating as far back as the eighteen hundreds. In no time at all, their avid quarrying had transformed the shapeless sacks into bulging barrels, and when the ledger-face had been exhausted, Mr Laurence unearthed a seam of old newspapers (including, no doubt, one with crosses pencilled down the length of the domestic vacancies column, and another with his own name correctly spelt with a 'u'). Frankie and Jim were jubilant. Was it that day, more than any other, that sealed young Kitchener's love for the sweet-shop that eventually, with a good deal of financial backing and encouragement from Miss Dill, became his very own, thriving concern? Did the mysterious characters contained in the yellowing account books weave some kind of spell when he was exposed to them (a spell that not even the Bard's characters had managed to weave)?

Told by Lloyd George that "Britain must be put in the way to feed herself", and touched by Dora's everpotent wand, the new Board of Agriculture duly took possession of as many acres of land as it could get its hands on. It was a spectacular success. Any farmer deemed to be inefficient was ousted, and land that had fallen into disuse as a result of the drain of workers into the army was given a new lease of life by industrious prisoners of war, conscientious objectors, teams of children, and, last but not least, the 260,000-strong Women's Land Army.

The Great War on Want (a plot within a plot often overlooked by theatre critics) had reached a truly significant point. The gardens, tennis courts, parks and schoolfields cultivated for vegetables under the war-cry "Idle Land for Food" could provide only so much. The time had come to bring millions of extra acres under the plough, and it was heralded by a new battle-cry: GROW MORE. And so it was that, prompted by the PM; empowered by the Mighty D, the Board of Agriculture hurled itself into the fray. Endless furrows were opened up overnight, but unlike those across the waters, they were sown with seeds, not men. Thanks entirely to the efforts of the Board, the nation was soon able to wrap itself in a mantle of green: the Colour of Growth. The British countryside was again a joy to behold. Yet, immeasurably more important than its effect on the eye (and even on the stomach come the harvest) was its effect on the nation's sense of smell. It is a well-known fact that when the wind blew from the south-east, it was often tinged with the bitter-sweet scent of human carrion. The public at large could put up with fearing that their loved ones might be killed; they could even put up with finding out that they had, but to put up with the stench of their rotting remains... Morale would have crumbled. The Grand Production would have lost its mass appeal. In short, the repercussions would have been disastrous. However, as acre upon acre of fertile soil sprouted into colourful life, the Albion air was filled with an invigorating fragrance of such richness that the tainted south-easterlies swept by largely undetected. The noses-that-be were thus able to breathe a little easier.

But despite its ostensible commitment to the belief that, after all is said and done, Man lives primarily by bread (whether it be made of potato or bean flour), the very nature of the Board's greatest contribution betrays an acute awareness than Man does not, in fact, live by it alone.

Wassat noise? *What* noise? *That* noise! Ah! It's the politicians sharpening their knives. Politicians? Knives? *'Course*: it's all over bar the shouting, and the cake's about to be cut. Cake? *What* cake? *Europe*, you fool!

It is a reception fit for kings, even though the vast majority of them happen to be pawns. Assuming the role of a Buckingham Palace or a Westminster Abbey, stands the Charing Cross Hotel, every one of its windows peopled by excited on-lookers. Instead of a royal cavalcade, there is a long procession of slow-moving ambulances, their sides and tops emblazoned with a red cross on a white background. But the cheering, waving crowds are very much themselves, flanking the procession in their thousands. Soldiers in uniform also line the route, saluting the motorised floats laden with khakied, bandaged men. Policemen doing their duty as inconspicuously as they can, ensure that the number of civilians who try shaking a wounded hand, or present a small bouquet, is kept to a respectable minimum. Men in boaters, bowlers and caps observe the goings-on with glowing pride, while women here and there sob openly into embroidered handkerchiefs.

The clan has gathered by the gateway to the railway station. Behind them is the Underground entrance; opposite, a Bureau de Change buckling under the weight of people perched on and around its main hoarding. Every single member of the family is present. Old and young have been present and waiting for the past four days. Ambulances approach them, ambulances pass by. Each one a hope of reunion; each one, so far, a disappointment. From morning to evening, they wait, until the procession runs dry. Today, however, the general consensus of intuitions is that they shall not be let down again. The first lorryful of the day can be heard coming towards the gateway. A loud cheer goes up all around them. Soldiers stand to attention. Policemen stretch out their arms... No. Hope turns to disappointment to hope as the next one follows... No. Only the small members of the clan voice the occasional doubt; question the need to wait, wait, wait...

"Mum! Dad!"

Newly-disappointed eyes have already set their hopeful sights on the ambulance behind. The clan looks back and gasps in disbelief before crying out his name. He waves, leaning out of the front of the ambulance as far as he can. As one, they push past the not-long-enough arms of the law and easily catch up the vehicle. No star has ever been so embraced and hugged and kissed and embraced again; no adoring fans have ever wept so profoundly. At the emotional height of the reunion, a boy is hoisted in the air and passed into the arms of his father. The child stares at the half-bandaged face and bursts into tears. The clan laughs, wiping away its own. After clutching his son to his chest for a few, long seconds, the man hands him back. Almost too overcome to speak, he manages to shout out, "They're takin' me to St Matthew's, in 'Arlesden."

The ambulance is allowed to speed into the Strand.

To the indescribable relief of his family, Jack Kitchener returned home in March, 1918. He was the victim, if that is the right word, of a Blighty wound: the kind that ends your active service but not your life, and, together with the apparition of Rose, the story of how it happened became a piece of Kitchener-esque folklore.

"There were Germans all roun' us, an' they were closin' in fast. After years of 'oldin' the fron' we were ordered t'retrea'. You couldn' 'ear a thing for field guns. Every time one of theirs came over, the 'ole earth shook, an' once I saw a direct 'it on one of our guns. The 'ole lo' wen' up in a cloud of smoke...bits of men, 'orses, metal... It was jus' after tha' the bomb wen' off. Mustta been a good ten fee' away. All I remember's this grea' force throwin' me ter the groun'. I didn' feel any pain, tha' came la'er. The M.O. took one look at me an' said there was nothin' 'e could do. 'Looks like you've been skinned,' 'e said. So they sen' me ter the C.C.S., stuck me on a train, an' pu' me in an 'ospi'al for a couple of weeks. Tha's when I go' evacua'ed."

In the cold, coal-rationed Kitchener household, the wounded hero recounted his adventures to a captivated audience (among which was occasionally to be found Miss Dill and, of course, an ageing brother-in-law banished to bachelorhood – albeit very discreetly). Waited on by Lady and his sisters, but especially by Elisabeth, the convalescent would tell of the many friends he had lost, the hardship, the moments of humour, and, with affectionate pride, the way that Fred, against all the odds, had earnt himself the Albert Medal.

"No one knew at the time they'd give 'im an A.M. for it. All the men in our company came an' shook 'is 'and when they foun' out abou' it. Any'ow, this is wha' 'appened. We were marchin' back to billets after our stint in the trenches when we foun' this RHA 'orse, 'alf buried in frozen mud. It was still alive. Our commandin' officer took 'is gun out t'pu' it ou' of its misery. Course, Fred wouldn' 'ear of it. You know 'ow 'e loves 'orses. So 'e tells the officer 'e's an exper' on 'orses, an' volun'eers t'do the job 'imself, an' then bury it 'imself. Nine times ou' of ten, the officer wouldn've taken any notice an' sho' it there an' then. This time, though, 'e pu' 'is gun away an' tol' someone t'give Fred a shovel. Then we marched off an' lef' 'im on 'is own in the freezin' cold. Typical of Fred, instead've shootin' it an' buryin' it, 'e shovelled all the ice away an' go' it ou', jus' t'see if it was lame. Took 'im hours. It's a miracle 'e didn' freeze t'death, an' 'ow tha' 'orse pu' up with the cold I'll never know. Fred must've known by the look in its eye or somethin' tha' it was really all righ', cos it *was*! After get'in' it ou', 'e checked for broken bones an' couldn' fine any, so 'e rubbed its body all over t'ge' the blood goin' again. When 'e was sure the 'orse could manage it, 'e led it back t'billets ... Firs' thin' our commandin' officer did was t'shou' 'is 'ead off at 'im for disobeyin' orders an' riskin' 'is life for nothin'. Nex' thin' we know, 'e's up for a medal! Some of the men nick-named 'im Sain', after St Francis... I 'ope 'e's all righ' still."

Unbeknown to them all, Fred *was* all right, and destined, in years to come, to help Frank Kitchener (Jnr) with the running of the shop at 221 High Road Kilburn. Edward too would return safe and well, and although he would father another three children, none ever came close to hatching out of their mother's womb on Christmas Day – besides, they were all boys, so, perhaps, it was just as well.

By mid-spring, Jack had told them everything (or nearly everything) that there was to tell, and whether they realised it or not, the informal audiences conducted in those pre-Armistice days of 1918 were of invaluable therapeutic worth. He had relived and shared his most memorable experiences in their company, a moving process that went a long way to lightening the burden of his immediate past: his stay in an old convent; his march to the farmhouse where the company was to be billeted; his baths in buckets of cold water; his baths in steaming vats; his exposure to arctic weather conditions, and to the trench-stench of death in the summer months; his respect for the German soldier; his lack of respect for the French in matters of hygiene; his encounter with Rose; his shooting of a young sniper; his sorrow after Corporal Talbot was killed in action...all these gradually became theirs. However, this constituted only one half of the equation, for they too had been separated from him during all those years, so, one by one, they invited him to partake of their respective versions of life at home in the shadow of war: the shortage of essentials; the endless queuing; the soaring tax levels; the black-outs; the air raids; the growing number of war-industry strikes; the riots; the silenced church bells...

Then, collectively, but only after his burns and state of mind gave them no further cause for worry, they told him that Mary, George, Hubert and Thomas were no longer with them, and having stoked up the painful cinders of grief, mourned their deaths anew.

Epitaph

MCMXIV-MCMXVIII

11th November. Down comes the curtain. Up go the hands: rapturous applause; standing ovation – but *please*, no cries of 'Encore!'

Weshallremember. The Cenotaph, that towering Empty Tomb; that magnificent Academy Award; that huge Quarried Phallus in Whitehall stands erect – to be unveiled.

Heupstagedher. The long-awaited moment has finally arrived, but on whom does the spotlight fall? On the Unknown Extra! Foaming at the mouth, Dora flees the boards never to return – *never?*

****

War fever marked the beginning of hostilities. An equally fatal fever marked their suspension. Spawned, in all probability, in the rat and lice-infested trenches of western Europe, Spanish Influenza claimed some twenty-million lives throughout the world between 1918 and 1919.

Two of those lives belonged to Jack and Elisabeth Kitchener, who died within days of each other in October, 1918. Regrettably, not even all the king's bishops and all the king's horses, let alone all the unSistine-like fingers on all the posters in all the kingdom, could put them (or anybody else) together again.

Ashes to ashes, infinitesimal specks of dust to dust...